GREAT MARLOW

Parish and People in the Nineteenth Century

By

MARTEN

Edited by **JEAN M COOK**

Published by Marten
c/o Dr Rachel Brown, High Rews Farm, Marlow, SL7 3DD

Designed by Eric Thompson
Printed by Parchment (Oxford) Limited, Oxford

Cover illustration: Reproduction of an original painting of Marlow showing the old church, the wooden bridge built in 1790, the barn and the house now known as Thames Lawn; the original is in the possession of
Mrs E.A. White.
Photograph by Brian Drage

CONTENTS

FOREWORD

It is with great pleasure that I welcome this major piece of Marlow's local history. This reconstruction of the town and its people in the mid-nineteenth century arises from the work of a University extramural class which met in Marlow between 1987 and 1990. The class was tutored by Miss Jean Cook of Oxford University Department for Continuing Education, and was organized in conjunction with the Marlow Adult Education Centre of Buckinghamshire County Council.

The purpose of OUDCE is to extend opportunities for study and research beyond the walls of a major, but sometimes remote-seeming, university. Local history is a subject which particularly offers chances for original investigation in a field where academic research and the wider, national historical picture can go hand in hand with the unique contribution made by local knowledge and enthusiasm. This is exactly what has happened in Marlow and it is an immense satisfaction to see a collaboration between university and local historians bear such worthwhile fruit. This has only been possible through the skill, knowledge and commitment of time and energy that Jean Cook as tutor of the group has provided. When first asked to undertake the task by myself and by those who knew and admired her earlier teaching in Marlow, Jean was characteristically modest at the prospect of venturing outside her usual periods of study. I, and all the members of the group with whom she has worked, are relieved and happy that she allowed herself to be persuaded to begin the research, and it will be clear that she and her students have made the subject their own. Rachel Brown, Mary Cowling, Peter Diplock, Valerie Evans, Pamela Galloway, Bob Loe, Bill Purser, Joan Rogers and Sheila Warne have all worked with Jean to research, write and produce the present volume.

The result is a wide-ranging picture of the life of Marlow in the mid-nineteenth century. The town, the wider parish, and the river are all explored. Schools and schooling, work and leisure, farming, the lively parliamentary and local politics of the period, the poor and how they were treated, the brewery, the many pubs, inns and ale-houses will all be encountered in the pages of this study. A major example of how to link carefully and painstakingly the available contemporary sources to repopulate, sometimes house by house, the homes and workplaces of a local community is provided. Readers interested in the nineteenth century, in small towns, or in Marlow in particular will all find much of interest in its pages. I am delighted to congratulate Jean Cook and her fellow historians on producing this admirable study.

KATE TILLER
University Lecturer in Local History
Oxford University Department for Continuing Education

ACKNOWLEDGEMENTS

This account of Marlow in the mid-nineteenth century grew out of an evening class run under the aegis of Oxford University's Department for External Studies (as it then was) and in collaboration with the Local Education Authority. Meetings were held in Great Marlow School during the winters of 87/88, 88/89 and 89/90.

We started by analysing all the information contained in the census enumerators' returns for Great Marlow, as it was then called, in 1851; then various members of the class became interested in particular topics such as politics, the vestry, agriculture and the workhouse. After the formal classes had finished some of the members decided that they wanted to continue working together informally with a view to publishing their findings and this book is the result. We hope that it is of interest both to long-established residents of the town and also to newcomers. We have tried to produce a readable text which also does justice to the considerable research undertaken by various people and we have deliberately included a large number of illustrations and newspaper cuttings.

We used the information in the 1851 census returns and our methodology is described in more detail at the start of the first section, but for those who have not used material like this before it is worth stressing that it can sometimes be difficult to interpret and even to read. The enumerators recorded what the householders said about themselves and their families and we cannot be sure of the difference between, for example, a cordwainer and a shoemaker or even whether any difference was intended. But despite such anomalies the returns provide a wealth of detailed information and we have used this to examine the social structure of the town at the time.

The rest of the book consists of a series of studies of different aspects of the life of Great Marlow, concentrating on the period around 1851 but sometimes going back in time where this seemed desirable in order to explain the background. Some of the people who turn up as farmers, ale-house keepers, craftsmen and tradesmen will already be familiar from the repopulation study and, wherever possible, we have tried to refer back to this. At the end of each section we have listed some of the sources of information which have been used.

This is by no means an exhaustive account and we are conscious that there is more work still to do. We hope that people who read this book and who can add more information will contact one of the authors so that the history of Marlow can continue to be recorded.

We have had help from a very large number of people; in particular we would like to thank:

Mary Adams
Linda Babb
Berkshire County Council Library staff at Maidenhead, Reading and Slough
The Headmaster of Sir William Borlase School
Bodleian Library
Grace Briggs
British Library, London
Buckinghamshire County Council Library staff at Aylesbury, High Wycombe and Marlow
Buckinghamshire County Record Office staff at Aylesbury
Hugh Butler

Mark Carlisle and Messrs. Simmons and Lawrence
Alan Coster
Molly Cox
Dilys Davies
Guildhall Library, London
Hugh Hanley
Mary Hodges
Enid Light
Marlow Society
Raine Morgan
Oxfordshire County Council, Centre for Oxfordshire Studies
Gordon Palmer
Peter Peters
Andrew Pike
Grace Price
Public Record Office
Nicholas Redman
Trudy Reeves
Royal Agricultural Society of England library staff
Shirley Stokes
Eric Thompson
Kate Tiller
Anthony Wethered
Vera Williams
David Wilson
Wycombe District Council
All the members of the original class, without whose careful work in transcribing the census returns the book could never have been written.

For help with the illustrations our thanks are due to:

Buckinghamshire County Museum
Buckinghamshire Record Office
Peter Diplock
Brian Drage
Alan Holmes
Institute of Agricultural History & Museum of English Rural Life
Marlow Library
Marlow Parochial Church Council
Marlow Society
National Museum of Wales
Oxfordshire Archives
Bill Purser
Margaret Richardson
Joan Rogers
Royal Commission on the Historical Monuments of England
Royal Pharmaceutical Society of Great Britain
Robert Ticehurst
J.H. Venn, S.H. Freese collection

Finally this book could not have been published without the generous financial support which we have received from the following individuals and institutions:

Kenneth Balfour
Francis Coales Charitable Foundation
Equity & Law Life Assurance PLC
Marc Fitch Fund
Folley Bros.
John Hester
Marlow Society
Platts of Marlow
Rank Xerox Limited
SAS Software Ltd.
Kenneth Spivey
Twenty-Seven Foundation
Whitbread PLC

At a critical stage G.J. White, of Widmere Farm, very generously undertook to meet any shortfall in the grants we received. This meant that we could go ahead with the printing in time to publish our book in 1991, a census year, and that we have not needed to take out a loan. This, in turn, has ensured that the book can be on sale at a reasonable price and that the proceeds can be used to support further work on the history of Great Marlow. All the authors and the editor are particularly grateful to Mr White for his support.

JEAN M. COOK

Population and Repopulation

In 1851 Great Marlow, as it was then called, was a small compact town, lying at the southernmost end of a parish of the same name. The size and shape of the parish, as shown in the 1843 Tithe Apportionment Map, were very similar to its present form. The major difference was the inclusion of Lane End, which was subsequently formed into a separate ecclesiastical parish in 1867, together with areas from other parishes; it became a separate civil parish in 1895 or 96.

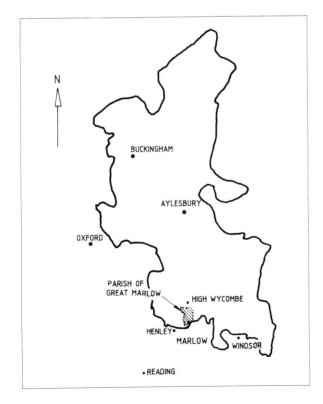

The county of Buckinghamshire showing the position of the parish and town of Great Marlow. Drawn by Joan Rogers

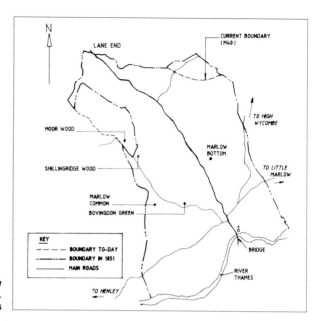

The parish of Great Marlow showing the 1851 boundary. Drawn by Joan Rogers

As the map shows the southern boundary of the parish ran along the Thames as far as Harleyford, at that time the site of the manor house occupied by the lord of the manor Sir William Robert Clayton, and then ran northwards to include Marlow Common and Moor Common in Lane End. Strangely, a detached portion of the parish of Lewknor (Oxfordshire) intruded on this line so that parts of the Frieth Road and Finnemore were not then in Great Marlow parish as they are now. In the east the boundary was the Wycombe Road as far as Handy Cross and Booker, so that Limmers, Holmers, Clay Lane and Barmoor were included. This line has only recently been modified since the building of the M40 and the modern civil parish excludes Holmers and anything north of the motorway. The ecclesiastical parish now contains Marlow town and all of the Great Marlow civil parish.

In 1851, Great Marlow was a parliamentary borough sending two members to Westminster and also served as a market town for the surrounding villages. It had no direct rail link then, the nearest station being at Maidenhead on the Great Western Railway; daily

2

connections were made by horse-drawn coach and there were carriers to other neighbouring towns.

The town's commercial activity centred on the paper mills, situated on the river bank, and on the two breweries. Both industries gave employment to a number of Marlow's inhabitants. Other trade was in corn, coal and timber, the river having provided a valuable route for transport of these goods until the advent of the railway. Barge traffic would have been a common sight in the early nineteenth century and some men still gave their occupation as bargeman or barge carter. Many women, on the other hand, were employed in lace-making or in satin-stitch work, both trades probably providing the opportunity for them to work from home.

The aim of this part of the study has been to build up a detailed picture of the centre of the town as it was in the mid-nineteenth century in order to examine its character and social structure. The main source of information was the census enumerators' returns for 1851. The census was taken on the night of Sunday 30 March in that year and all heads of household were required to record details of every person present on that night. The *Reading Mercury* for Saturday 15 March 1851 included the following:

> *The Census. In the course of a few days the schedules will be placed in the hands of every householder, to be filled up with every particular respecting the inhabitants of every dwelling on the night of March 30th that the appointed officers may receive them on March 31st. Any person refusing to give correct information will be liable to a penalty of five pounds, any misstatement of age or any particular will be equally liable. The Columns must all be filled in by the morning of the 31st.*

The information to be provided included age, sex, whether single, married or widowed, relationship to the head of the household, occupation and place of birth. Analysis of this basic data gives a wealth of information about the inhabitants of the town.

According to the census returns the population of Great Marlow in 1851 was 4,423, excluding people

INSTRUCTIONS for filling up the Column headed "RANK, PROFESSION, or OCCUPATION."

The Superior Titles of PEERS and other PERSONS or RANK to be inserted, as well as any high office which they may hold. Magistrates, Aldermen, and other important public officers to state their profession after their official title.

ARMY, NAVY, AND CIVIL SERVICE.—Add after the rank, "Army," "Artillery," "Royal Navy," "Marines," "East India Company's Service," as the case may be—distinguishing those on half-pay. Persons in the CIVIL SERVICE to state the Department to which they are attached, after their title or rank ; those on the Superannuation List to be so distinguished. Chelsea, Greenwich, and other Pensioners, to be clearly designated.

CLERGYMEN of the Church of England to return themselves as "Rector of——," "Vicar of ——," "Curate of ——," &c., or as not having cure of souls. They are requested not to employ the indefinite term "Clerk." Presbyterian Ministers and Roman Catholic Priests, to return themselves as such, and to state the name of the church or chapel in which they officiate. Dissenting Ministers to return themselves as "Independent Minister of —— Chapel," "Baptist Minister of —— Chapel," &c. Local or occasional preachers must return their ordinary occupations.

LEGAL PROFESSION.—Barristers, to state whether or not in actual practice ; Officers of any Court, &c., to state the description of office and name of Court. The designation "Attorney" or "Solicitor" to be confined to those whose names are actually upon the Roll. Persons in Solicitors' offices should distinguish whether "Solicitor's Managing, Articled, Writing, or General Clerk."

Members of the MEDICAL PROFESSION to state the University, College, or Hall, of which they are Graduates, Fellows, or Licentiates—also whether they practice as Physician, Surgeon, or General Practitioner, or are "not practising."

PROFESSORS, TEACHERS, PUBLIC WRITERS, Authors, and Scientific men—to state the particular branch of Science or Literature which they teach or pursue ; Artists, the branch they cultivate. Graduates should enter their degrees in this column.

PERSONS ENGAGED IN COMMERCE, as Merchants, Brokers, Agents, Clerks, Commercial Travellers, to state the particular kind of business in which they are engaged, or the staple in which they deal

The term FARMER to be applied only to the occupier of land, who is to be returned—"Farmer of [317] acres employing [12] labourers ;" the number of acres, and of in and out-door labourers, on March 31st, being in all cases inserted. Sons or daughters employed at home or on the farm, may be returned —"Farmer's Son," "Farmer's Daughter."

In TRADES the Master is to be distinguished from the Journeyman and Apprentice, thus— (Carpenter—Master employing [6] men) ;" inserting always the number of persons of the trade in his employ on March 31st.

In the case of WORKERS IN MINES OR MANUFACTURES, and generally in the constructive ARTS the particular branch of work, and the material, are always to be distinctly expressed if they are not implied in the names, as in Coal-miner, Brass-founder, Wool-carder, Silk-throwster. Where the trade is much sub-divided, both trade and branch are to be returned thus—"Watchmaker—Finisher ;" "Printer—Compositor."

A person following MORE THAN ONE DISTINCT TRADE may insert his occupations in the order of their importance.

MESSENGERS, PORTERS, LABOURERS, and SERVANTS, to be described according to the place and nature of their employment.

Persons following no Profession, Trade or calling, and holding no public office, but deriving their incomes chiefly from land, houses, mines, or other real property, from dividends, interest of money, annuities, &c. may designate themselves "Landed Proprietor," "Proprietor of Iron Mines," "Proprietor of Houses," "Fund-holder," "Annuitant," &c., as the case may be. Persons of advanced age who have RETIRED FROM BUSINESS to be entered thus—"Retired Silk Merchant," "Retired Watchmaker," &c.

ALMSPEOPLE, and persons in the receipt of parish relief should, after being described as such, have their previous occupations inserted.

WOMEN AND CHILDREN.—The titles or occupations of ladies who are householders to be entered according to the above Instructions. The occupations of women who are regularly employed from home, or at home, in any but domestic duties, to be distinctly recorded. So also of children and young persons. Against the names of children above five years of age, if daily attending school, or receiving regular tuition under a master or governess at home, write "Scholar," and in the latter case add "at home."

Part of the schedule issued to individual householders in 1851

sleeping rough and in boats. This was almost evenly divided:

Men and boys	Women and girls	Overall total
2153	2270	4423

There were six separate census areas and the following table sets out the details of these and the population distribution.

4

Census area	Area covered	Enumerator	Population M	F
1	High Street (west side),Bridge, Court Garden, Potlands, West Street, Hayes Place, Quoiting Place, Oxford Terrace, Oxford Lane	William Gregory	460	537
2	High Street (east side), Causeway, Churchyard, Church Passage, The Bridge, St.Peter's Street, Thames Bank, The Mills, Pound House, Mill Cottage, Mill Lane, Strong Beer Acre, Chapel Street	William Gibbons	509	575
3	Dean Street, Gas House, Marefield, Hatch's Row, Gun Lane, Gun Place, Common Slough, Crown Hotel, Market Street, Crown Lane, Spittal Street, Quoiting Place, Oxford Lane	Henry Badger	643	649
4	Towns End Cottage, Highfield, Beech Lodge, Red Pits, Low Ground Farm, Temple Pound, Harleyford, Tencrofts, Hooks, Marlow Common, Bovingdons Green, Forty Green and Spinfields	Thomas Bowen	174	164
5	Prospect House, Burrows Grove, Handy Cross, Homers, Old House, Ragman's Castle, Wymers, Juniper Hill, Marlow Bottom, White Hill, Seymours, High Rews, Copy Farm, Munday Dean and the late workhouse	Henry Stallwood	140	129
6	Hawkins Farm, Bismere Pond, Moor Common, Ditchfield, Lane End, Becking, Red Barn, Barmoor Farm, Clay Lane, Limmers Farm, Dirty Bottom, Widmere Farm and Cold Harbour	Edwin Seagrave	227	216
		Overall	2153	2270

All the enumerators were local men and their names will turn up again in other contexts during this study.

A second source was the parish Rate Book for the same year, compiled on 26 June, recording the amounts to be paid that year towards the repayment of the sum borrowed to finance the rebuilding of the parish church. The preamble reads:

> *A **RATE OR ASSESSMENT** of one shilling in the pound on the full annual*

Rent or Value of the Houses, Warehouses Shops Buildings Lands Tenements and Hereditaments rated or rateable for the relief of the Poor of the Parish of Great Marlow in the County of Bucks on all and every the Tenants or Occupiers of the said Parish made in pursuance of an Act of Parliament passed in the First year of the reign of King William the 4[t] intituled 'An Act for taking down the Parish Church of Great Marlow in the County of Buckinghamshire and for rebuilding the same on or near the present site thereof for the purpose of paying one years interest from the 14th February 1851 to the 14th February 1852 of the sums borrowed under and by virtue of the said Act and not less than the fortieth part of the principal and for other purposes according to the directions of the said Act.

Part of a page from the parish Rate Book

The value of the Rate Book is that, apart from being a useful cross-check on the occupants of the houses at the time, it gives details of the owners, a brief description of their property and its estimated value for purposes of calculating how much each occupier had to pay.

These two sources were usually supplemented by

The start of the classified section of the Musson and Craven Directory for 1853

information from the various Directories of the period. In many ways these are very useful but it is worth pointing out that they were usually out of date by the time they were published and they were by no means complete.

In order to try to repopulate the town as it would have been in 1851 it was necessary to work with a large scale map. This meant using the first edition Ordnance Survey map (1876), surveyed on a scale of 1:500. Although this is an accurate map and one which shows each individual building, it was not published until twenty-five years after the information collected from the census returns. In the intervening period some houses were built and others pulled down and in some cases whole areas were developed as, for example, with the arrival of the railway in 1873; sometimes new roads have been built, like Institute Road off High Street, and these have destroyed earlier properties. The Tithe Apportionment map, dated 1843, was useful in terms of identifying owners and occupiers of areas of land or larger properties, but it does not identify houses and gardens individually in the heart of the town.

Even with all this data, it is by no means straightforward to repopulate the houses shown on the map with the families which the census returns and other sources suggest were living there. The numbers on the census enumerators' returns are not street numbers but schedule numbers. So it is not always clear in which order houses were recorded. Sometimes more than one family lived in the same house, a detail which can be detected from the census returns but which was not always easy to spot. Cross-checking with the parish Rate Book proved useful in these cases. The Rate Book also provided the opportunity to compare values and sizes of properties, sometimes useful when trying to pin down a particular house.

The attempts at repopulation had to take all these limitations into account. One encouraging factor is that many of the houses in the centre of Marlow retain their nineteenth-century appearance from first floor upwards, even if the ground floors of the fronts are greatly altered, and, in a lot of cases, the backs of the houses are even earlier. In addition the width of the individual street frontages as they would have been in 1851 can usually be clearly seen, even though modern shop fronts may have amalgamated two or more properties at ground floor level. This means that these buildings, identifiable today, can sometimes be repopulated with the people who were living in them in 1851. When the intervening history of the property is also known it is sometimes possible to trace continuity of use over some or all of the 140 years. In practice it was only possible to be certain about the occupancy of a small number of houses in some of the streets which were studied and we have included sections of the map to illustrate these. But, despite discrepancies, the intimate knowledge which was gained about the population of these streets proved very valuable in trying to recreate Great Marlow as it was in the mid-nineteenth century.

To attempt to repopulate the whole town was beyond the scope of this study. In the end we worked on High Street, St Peter's Street, Spittal Street, Chapel Street, Dean Street and West Street. The overall impression is of a small town which, although not declining at a rapid rate, was not expanding at a fast rate either. Population growth was very slow during the whole of the nineteenth century. Figures show that in England and Wales the population doubled between 1801 and 1851 and then doubled again by about the end of the century. In marked contrast the population of the county of Buckinghamshire did not double from the 1801 figure until 1911, while the population of Marlow, which was 3,240 in 1801, did not double until 1951.

Other towns in Buckinghamshire show a different trend. Aylesbury had doubled its 1801 population by 1871, as might be expected for what was by then the

Changes in population 1801-1951 in Great Marlow

Year	Population	Intercensal change	% increase/decrease
1801	3240		
1811	3970	+730	+22.53
1821	3760	−210	− 5.28
1831	4240	+480	+12.76
1841	4480	+240	+ 5.66
1851	4423	− 57	− 1.27
1861	4660	+237	+ 5.35
1871	4700	+ 40	+ 0.86
1881	4760	+ 60	+ 1.28
1891	5250	+490	+10.29
1901	5650	+400	+ 7.62
1911	5320	−330	− 5.84
1921	5140	−180	− 3.38
1931	5280	+140	+ 2.72
1941	no national census taken		
1951	6840		

county town. Wycombe increased its population by four and a half times in the nineteenth century, while Upton-cum-Chalvey, later to be Slough, expanded by more than nine times. The graph shows this very clearly.

One of the main reasons for this disparity of growth must be related to the advent of the railway. It reached Maidenhead and Slough in 1838, though the latter station was not built until 1840. Maidenhead, in Berkshire, was the nearest station to Marlow and in 1851 it was to Maidenhead that people went to travel by train. There were proposals to bring the railway to Marlow in the 1860s. Colonel Brownlow Knox, one of the borough's MPs, supported the scheme in 1864 but when up for re-election in 1866 he changed his mind. As a result the railway did not reach the town until 1873, by which time other towns had expanded and Marlow was left behind.

We have not made a close study of places of birth but, because all our data has been computerised, we are able to make one or two very general comments. Three quarters of the population, roughly 3,300 people, were born within the county of Buckinghamshire. Coming closer to home, about 1,400 males and 1,360 females were actually born in the parish itself. These last two figures

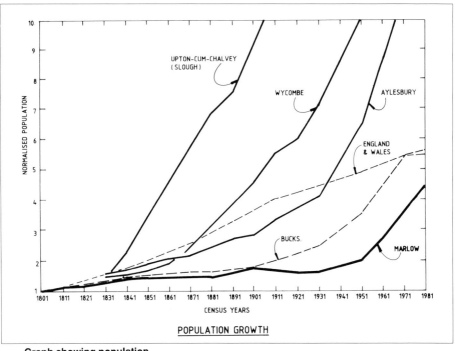

POPULATION GROWTH

Graph showing population growth in Great Marlow compared with that for the nation, the county and other selected towns. Drawn by Joan Rogers

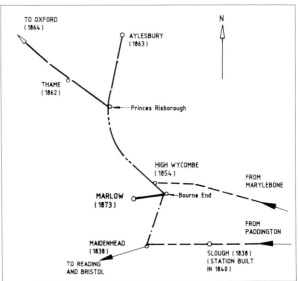

Simplified map to illustrate the development of the railway. Drawn by Joan Rogers

10

included about 80% of all children under the age of fourteen.

The range of occupations suggests that Marlow was self-sufficient for goods and services. The affairs of the town seem to have been run by a relatively small group of shopkeepers and craftsmen. There is no real evidence of an upper class, apart from a handful of citizens described as gentry, and no substantial group to provide the town with political or other leadership. The main streets of the town all show to a greater or lesser extent the same mix of traders/craftsmen and labourers, often living in close proximity. Additional evidence to show that many of the families were Great Marlow born and bred is provided by the recurrence of the same surnames, often in the same street, and this suggests close relationships within the town. Confirmation of this is sometimes visible in the Christian names of children, who seem to have been named after aunts or uncles. Many of the surnames recorded in the census returns are still common in the

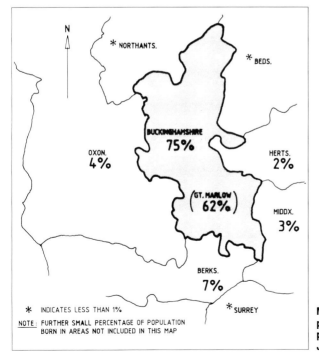

Map showing birth-places of people living in Great Marlow parish in 1851. Drawn by Joan Rogers

11

All Saints Church and the entrance to the bridge, 1859. Rock & Co London No 4099

Tithe barn, probably belonging to Bisham Abbey, as it appeared in about 1880. The original barn was 'in the style of the early part of Edward I' with thirteenth-century lancet windows. By the mid-nineteenth century it had become very dilapidated. Photograph by H.W. Taunt, reproduced by courtesy of Buckinghamshire County Museum town today. These include Batting, Bowles, Coster, Creswell, Cresswell, Gibbons, Lovegrove, Oxlade, Plumridge, Rockell, Salmon, Stroud, Truss, Wellicome and Wethered.

High Street

People entering Great Marlow over the bridge in 1851 would have come on foot, on horseback, by carriage, or by coach or carrier as the only public means of transport. The road surface, judging by early prints, was cobbled and there were footpaths for pedestrians. After 1848 the main streets would have been lit by gas lamps at night. Close to the bridge, on the site of the modern Tierney Court, stood the monastic tithe-barn, built of chalk, flint and stone rubble and probably being used as a coal store in 1851. It was pulled down some time after 1862 and its roof timbers were used in the rebuilding of the church at Lane End in 1878.

The old church of All Saints, pulled down about 1830. Reproduced by courtesy of the Royal Commission of the Historical Monuments of England

13

The Great Marlow parish church of All Saints had been rebuilt between 1832 and 1835. At the time of the census it would have consisted simply of a rectangular nave, with three entrances at the west end, a small tower and a spire. The vicarage at that time was about half way up the High Street, next to what is now the Post Office. About 1865 a new vicarage was built nearer the church on the site which in 1851 was occupied by an ale-house called The Swan, owned by the Wethered family, who were brewers. This later vicarage was modified in the 1960s and was finally replaced when a modern house was bought for the purpose in 1989. The Swan was kept by George Creswell, a member of a well-known Marlow family, who was also a timber-dealer employing nine men. Born in the town, George, who was forty-six in 1851, had three sons and two daughters, all born in the parish.

The Swan Inn, about 1860. The gateway on the left, with the dial, is still visible today. Reproduced by Brian Drage from a print owned by Margaret Smith. The original photograph was taken by H.W. Taunt

The family also had two lodgers. He seems to have been landlord of The Swan for at least ten years according to the local directories, from 1842 until 1853. The building of the vicarage on the site of his ale-house obviously meant that he had to move and the 1864 directory lists a George Creswell, farmer, barge-owner and coal-dealer, living in St Peter's Street. This is almost certainly the same man since the only one of his sons to be called George would only have been fourteen in 1864.

Going on up The Causeway, Dial Cottage was lived in in 1851 by Robert Collins and his wife Lucy. He was born in the parish but she came from Havant in Hampshire. They had one servant and Mr Collins was regarded as one of the gentry. He is listed under nobility, gentry and clergy in both the 1847 and 1851 directories and is described as a landholder in the Census. In spite of this he did not own his house but was a tenant of John Rolls, a coal-merchant who lived near the bridge.

Two doors up from Dial Cottage was another ale-house, the George and Dragon, also owned by Wethered. The licensee, John Hobbs, was eighty and was born in Medmenham; his wife Charlotte was fifty-four and came originally from Southampton. Their unmarried daughter Emily, aged twenty-three, was also living there. She was born in Holloway, Middlesex, suggesting that the family had spent some time in London before returning to John Hobbs's home area. Certainly the tavern was run by someone else in 1841 and by 1861 Hobbs had been replaced – almost certainly he had died by then.

The George and Dragon, c.1920, still on the same site today as in 1851 though now much extended. Photograph by H.W. Taunt, reproduced by courtesy of Buckinghamshire County Museum

The present Church Hall contains a brass plate recording that in 1851 schools were built on the site by Owen and Lawrence Wethered 'in fulfilment of the intentions of the late Thomas Wethered Esquire'. Part of

Inn sign of the George and Dragon. Photograph by Peter Diplock, 1991

the land was given for the purpose by the Dean and Chapter of Bristol, who had been granted lands in Marlow in 1542 by Henry VIII. Thomas's widow, Sarah, endowed the schools for 'the payment of the Master and Mistress of the Sunday Schools and other expenses in the management thereof'. The Wethered brothers established a fund to deal with repairs and insurance and the Trust deeds were enrolled in Chancery on 4 June 1852 and deposited with the Vicar and Churchwardens.

On the corner of The Causeway and Brook Street, now Station Road, lived James Bird Brooks, a baker; the same house still trades as a baker's, now being known as Burger's. James Brooks had been born in Great Marlow and his wife, Mary, came from Taplow. Their widowed daughter, Sarah Clifford, and her son William, aged five, lived with them. James and Mary also had a son of their own called William who lived there and worked as his father's assistant. The household had one servant. James Brooks also owned other houses in the immediate vicinity so it seems as if he was a man of some substance in the town.

On the west side of High Street, on the corner with Pound Lane, lived Esther Wright, aged sixty-six, a fund-holder of independent means. She was the widow

of John Snelling Wright who, before his retirement, was the senior partner in a firm of solicitors. Esther came from Shillingford and lived with her unmarried niece, also a fund-holder, and one servant.

William Lakin Ward lived next door in Brampton House. He was a solicitor in the same practice as Mr Wright and was very much involved in the affairs of the town. His signature can be seen on many of the surviving

I am,
Sir,
Your obedt. Servt,
W. L. Ward

William Lakin Ward's signature on a letter to Sir William Clayton dated 28 June 1851. The original is in Buckinghamshire County Record Office documents. He was Clerk to the Magistrates, Clerk to the Land Commissioners, Clerk to the Trustees of the Church Rate Account, Secretary to the Gas Works and Secretary to the Subscription News Room. Aged forty-four in 1851, he came from Chelmsford originally. He had married a Wendover girl, Jane, and they had a daughter of four and a son of eleven months, both born in Great Marlow; their household was completed by four servants. Mrs Ward lived to be ninety-four, ending her days in New Court, High Street, then a private house, with her son George, by then fifty-eight, as her companion. She had survived her energetic husband by thirty-six years. Incidentally, Mr Ward's payment to the Church Rate Account, as recorded in the Rate Book, was £1.1s.3d. He did not own his house but paid a rent of about £25 a year to the owner, Mr Davenport, who owned quite a lot of property in the town, including Esther Wright's house next door. Richard Davenport had been Sheriff for Buckinghamshire in 1789, in which year he bought Court Garden. He died ten years later and the property passed to the Davenport Bromley family.

New Court stables, now shops, and the entrance to Liston Court shopping area, 1991. Drawn by Margaret Richardson

A little further up, still on the west side of the High Street, lived John Smith, who had a shop there as well as his house. He was a china dealer, printer and bookseller, born in Great Marlow, who lived with his wife, who came from Suffolk, and their four sons and two daughters, aged between twelve and one. All the children were born in the parish and the three eldest sons and the six-year-old daughter were at school. John Smith paid a rent of £12 a

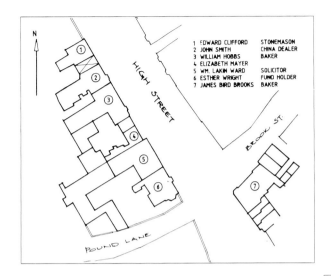

year to his landlord, Thomas Peers Williams, who owned a large number of houses in the town, including Marlow Place, and was one of the borough's two Members of Parliament. There is more about T.P.Williams in the section on politics.

Next to the Smiths, in Little Stone House, lived Edward Clifford, stone- and marble-mason, and his wife

Marlow Place, associated with Frederick, Prince of Wales (1707-51), in the 1730s. Drawn in 1991 by Margaret Richardson

Little Stone House, probably so called because Edward Clifford was a stonemason. Photograph by Peter Diplock, 1991

and brother, also a mason. The Rate Book shows that Clifford was assessed for a shed down on the wharf which suggests that some of his raw materials such as free-stone (any stone which can be cut and worked easily in any direction) arrived in Great Marlow by river. Edward and his brother were the sons of Theophilus Clifford who did the stonework for the suspension bridge and was also involved in reinstating the monuments in the newly-built church. Theophilus had a daughter baptised in the old parish church in 1829, the year in which the bridge was started, and she was christened Charlotte Suspensiana Clifford. She must have been Edward's sister.

Living at the Brewery at that time was Owen Wethered, oldest son of Thomas Wethered, the founder, who, as we have seen, had left instructions about the establishment of the church schools. Owen was fifty-two at the time of the census and his wife, Anne, who came from Accrington in Lancashire, was forty-four. They had, in all, twelve children, of whom six are recorded in the returns, and five servants. All the principal brewery buildings had been built by 1851, the most recent being the racking-cellar built against the north wall in 1826 and an extension to the brewhouse in 1832. The view through the front gates in 1851 would have been much as it is today as far as the buildings are concerned. Owen and Anne started their married life in The White House, the building with bow windows to the right of the entrance to the

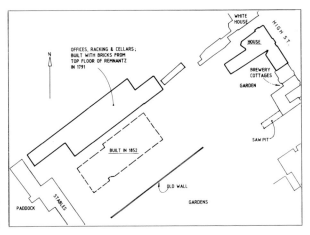

Plan of the brewery buildings as they were in 1851. Drawn by Joan Rogers

20

The White House, built in the late eighteenth century. The main entrance to the Wethered brewery is on the left. Reproduced by courtesy of Buckinghamshire County Museum

brewery, but, with their large family, may have moved into the Brewery House which was being used as living quarters at that date.

Owen had two brothers, Lawrence and Florence James. Lawrence, who was unmarried in 1851, was still living with his mother Sarah Wethered at Remnantz, the

The Brewery House, built in the eighteenth century, was lived in over the years by the Wethered family until it became the main offices of the brewery. Reproduced by courtesy of Buckinghamshire County Museum

family house in West Street called after Stephen Remnant who had lived there in the 1750s. Florence James was a clerk in holy orders and sometime vicar of Hurley. Owen and Lawrence were responsible for the running of the brewery after their father's death in 1849 and were employing some forty-seven men. Records show that the number of tied houses was about one hundred in 1851 and that only another twelve were acquired during the fifties, suggesting that the brewery's performance had reached a plateau by 1860 or so. Although the very even production levels and lower average profits suggest that Thomas's two sons were following their father's practice of not actively seeking new and wider markets, the brewery was undoubtedly a major employer in the town throughout the period with which we are concerned.

Next door to the Wethereds, and in a house owned by them, lived Joseph Wilkinson, aged forty-one, from Crofton in Leicestershire, and his wife and young son. Mr Wilkinson was a surgeon (MRCS) and the family had four

The Brewery House in 1991 showing the drawing-room extension on the left. This was added by Thomas Wethered c.1818, involving the demolition of two cottages, though the windows were a later insertion. Photograph by Bill Purser

servants. The census returns record that another surgeon, George Robson from Yorkshire, was visiting the Wilkinsons that day. The Musson and Craven Directory for 1853 lists both men as surgeons at the same address, so perhaps in 1851 Mr Robson had come to Great Marlow for an interview or had even just taken up a partnership. This is not mere idle speculation since there is a record in the *Gentleman's Magazine* of the death on 24 February 1851 of a William Trew, aged 36, who was a surgeon of Great Marlow. Perhaps Mr Robson was a replacement.

One or two houses further up lived Robert Maddocks, in a house owned by T.P.Williams and almost certainly on the site of the building now occupied by Lloyds Bank. Maddocks was an important man in Great Marlow, a master-builder aged sixty-four from Cheshire, whose wife was a local girl from Bisham. He was vicar's warden for 1851 and also a General Trustee of the Church Rate Account and often chaired vestry meetings. The 1853 Directory lists him as joiner, builder and county surveyor, and his property is described as a house, three stables, chaise house – for his carriages – garden, sheds and shops.

Across the road, on the east side of High Street and a little nearer the river, was The Chequers, an ale-house run by David Davis and owned by T.P.Williams. Davis was landlord for at least twenty years and came from Great Marlow. He and his wife Elizabeth had four children: Jane, eleven, John, seven, Owen, five, and Ellen, three. The two boys are described as scholars, but not Jane, the eldest – was she perhaps already helping in the tavern?

Between The Chequers and Cromwell House, once

Lloyds Bank in 1991. Property boundaries suggest that this is on the site of Robert Maddocks's house and, even earlier, the site of the 'Lower' Crown, from which stage-coaches ran. Photograph by Bill Purser

The Chequers inn sign. Photograph by Peter Diplock, 1991

Cromwell House in 1991. Earlier called Alfred House, this was the home of the Ellison family. Photograph by Bill Purser

23

the Post Office, was the house then used as the vicarage. At the time of the census it was uninhabited and the Reverend Frederick Bussell, who had only recently been appointed as vicar, is recorded as living opposite, possibly as a temporary lodger, with James Meeks, the veterinary surgeon. The vicar was thirty-two and married, but his wife is not recorded in the census. Perhaps she was still in their previous parish in March 1851. By the date of the Rate Book, almost three months later, the vicar's name appears as the next-door neighbour to Charles Bloxham, solicitor, who was living at Cromwell House.

Mr Bloxham was born in Highbury, Middlesex, but the family probably had a London house as well as one in Marlow; certainly the surname is known from a marriage in 1779. His wife Elizabeth came from Kent. Both were aged fifty and they had five children. Elizabeth, aged twenty-two, and Harriet, aged eighteen, were both at home and Anna, thirteen, John, seven, and Ann, six, were being educated at home by their governess Elizabeth Vaughan. The rest of the household consisted of a cook, a housemaid and a general house servant, all women, two of them from Norfolk and one from Wales. Mr Bloxham was assessed for an annual rent of £70 for his house and was also assessed for a pleasure ground and garden (£6) and a meadow (£3.17s.6d.) all in High Street. His house was owned by a Mrs Ellison. This family had in fact owned the house since earlier in the nineteenth century and the two families were associated through the partnership of Ellison and Bloxham, who were London solicitors for many years. Around 1800 the house was known as Alfred House and for much of the time during which the Royal Military College was based in the town it was rented out. The College was established in Marlow in 1799 and flourished there for just over ten years before its removal to Sandhurst in 1811. Several houses in the town were used as hostel accommodation and the main headquarters was at Remnantz.

Next to the Bloxhams lived George Kidd, a grocer and tea dealer, and then William Bond, born in Great Marlow and a bachelor. He paid an annual rent of £25 a year to T.P.Williams for his house. Presumably he is the man who had the contract for building All Saints Church – he must have been about thirty at the time. Bond's

premises were eventually acquired by Thomas Corby, who lived further up the High Street in 1851, and then, in 1876, by Young James Lovell. He was still renting the property at the time of the sale of the Williams's estate in 1905. The Kidds and William Bond each had one general servant.

Continuing on up the High Street on the east side were one or two smaller households like those of Richard and Kitty Way – he was a carpenter and is included in the Wethereds' wages list for 1858 when his wages were 18s. a week and she was a dressmaker – and Steadman Camden and his wife Catherine – he was a shoemaker and Mrs Camden was mistress of the 'blue girls' school' set up under the will of Sir William Borlase. More details of the school can be found in the section on education. The Ways' house was owned by Williams and the rent was £10 and the Camdens lived in a Wethered house and paid £12.

At the top end of the High Street on both sides of the road lived some of the relatively well-to-do shopkeepers – some of whom were key figures in the running of the town. On the right, at Number 1, lived Thomas Rolls, a draper and wine merchant. He was an unmarried man of sixty-one born in Great Marlow, who lived with his sisters Susan, who had never married, and Sophia who was a widow. Both ladies were fund-holders. Edward Wells, draper's assistant, lived in and there were two house servants. The house was owned by T.P.Williams and Mr

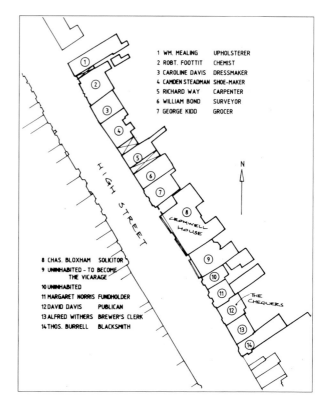

1 WM. MEALING   UPHOLSTERER
2 ROBT. FOOTTIT   CHEMIST
3 CAROLINE DAVIS   DRESSMAKER
4 CAMDEN STEADMAN   SHOE-MAKER
5 RICHARD WAY   CARPENTER
6 WILLIAM BOND   SURVEYOR
7 GEORGE KIDD   GROCER

N

HIGH STREET

CROMWELL HOUSE

THE CHEQUERS

8 CHAS. BLOXHAM   SOLICITOR
9 UNINHABITED - TO BECOME THE VICARAGE
10 UNINHABITED
11 MARGARET NORRIS   FUNDHOLDER
12 DAVID DAVIS   PUBLICAN
13 ALFRED WITHERS   BREWER'S CLERK
14 THOS. BURRELL   BLACKSMITH

Rolls paid £24.10s. a year in rent. It is possible to trace a connection from Mr Rolls, draper and wine merchant having premises with a 'furniture room' at the top of the High Street in 1851, via Rolls and Lawrence and later Lawrence Son and Laird, to Simmons and Lawrence, auctioneers and estate agents, at 1 High Street in 1990.

Next to him, in the house now occupied by the Halifax Building Society, was William Henry Brown, a pastry-cook, confectioner and grocer. The census records the next house as being empty; it was also owned by Williams and the rent was £20 a year. It now houses the National Westminster Bank. Then there was George Pearce, a hairdresser, stationer and bookseller. He came from Aylesbury, Buckinghamshire, and his wife Adelaide from Watlington in Oxfordshire. In their early thirties, the couple had three sons and a daughter, all born in Great

1-3 High Street, the home and place of work of Thomas Rolls. Drawn by Margaret Richardson, 1991

Marlow. It is perhaps worth commenting that Mr Pearce's apparently bizarre mix of occupations would have appeared quite normal in the mid-nineteenth century, when multiple trades were common. The Pearces' neighbours, in the house now occupied by Marlow Travel, were the Fullicks family, Thomas, grocer and tea dealer, and his wife Emma, both from Great Marlow, and their son Arthur, aged three. A grocer's assistant lived in and the family had one house servant. Both these houses, and that of William Brown, were owned by T.P.Williams.

George Cannon, who lived in the next house, currently occupied by Ashworths and Lees Bakery, was a bookseller, printer and chemist, who came from Maidenhead in Berkshire. His wife, Mary, who came from Middlesex, was fourteen years younger than her husband, and the couple had two daughters, one aged nine and the other eight months, and a son aged three. There were two servants and, again, a living-in assistant. Cannon paid an annual rent of £30 a year for his house, which was owned by Martha Aveling, and he also paid her £4 a year for a meadow; in addition the Rate Book says that he owned land in High Street. He was also assessed on 'half the tithe of Great Marlow Parish' which he was leasing from the Dean and Chapter of Gloucester. There is more about the

27

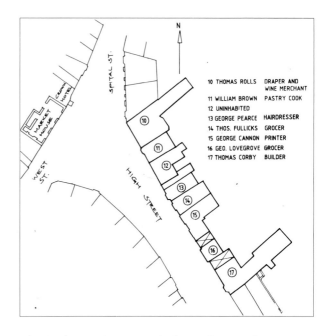

10 THOMAS ROLLS   DRAPER AND
                     WINE MERCHANT
11 WILLIAM BROWN   PASTRY COOK
12 UNINHABITED
13 GEORGE PEARCE   HAIRDRESSER
14 THOS. FULLICKS   GROCER
15 GEORGE CANNON   PRINTER
16 GEO. LOVEGROVE   GROCER
17 THOMAS CORBY   BUILDER

tithe in the section on agriculture. George Cannon was parish warden for 1851, elected at the same time as Robert Maddocks, and also chaired vestry meetings. The pair of them were responsible for the churchwardens' accounts for that year, of which there is more detail in the section on the church and vestry.

The other side of the High Street is more difficult to work out. The individual houses are less easy to identify on the map and this means that it is more difficult to be certain who lived where. Going up from James Meeks, the vet, were Edward August, a gardener and seedsman, and then Edward Hewett, a draper who employed four people. Hewett, who was forty, lived with his wife, their three children who were all under six, and their two servants, a cook and a nurse. The Marlow Horticultural Society held its annual show in the summer in Mr Hewett's meadow, as the following cutting from the *Windsor and Eton Express* on 14 June 1851 makes clear:

A report in the *Bucks Advertiser* on 5 July described the event, noting that 'a highly respectable and numerous party attended a first rate show'. Apparently the greenhouse plants were of the very first quality and the cottagers' table 'superceded all former years'. It was a fine day and the melodious strains of the band of the First Life Guards enlivened the scene, some 'first rate pieces being performed with beautiful effect'.

Mr Hewett's neighbour on the other side was Mary Ralfs, a retired draper who lived with her two sisters and a servant. The Misses Ralfs were members of the Salem Chapel, and owned several houses in the town. There were several traders and craftsmen including Thomas Anthony, butcher, Benjamin Gray, tailor, William Harding, shoemaker and James Maclean, brazier.

At the very top of the High Street lived William Pusey, a chair turner, and his wife who was a straw-bonnet maker. Also at that end of the street was George Hickman, who lived with his wife and two servants. Mr Hickman came from a well-known Marlow family; his father William Hickman, who had died in the previous year, had been a surgeon and George was also a qualified doctor but was no longer practising in 1851. Illustrations from the second half of the nineteenth century help to identify John Morgan's draper's shop and Robert Foottit's chemist's shop, but both families were living elsewhere at the time of the Census. The Foottits lived on the other side of the High Street, near to Steadman Camden and his wife, and the Morgan family lived in St Peter's Street. Morgan's continued as an outfitters for a long time, before becoming Daniels in the 1950s, and the building now houses offices and the Black Horse estate

Clark's shop in 1991. Two families lived in what were two separate houses in 1851; Robert Maddison was a butcher and almost certainly had a game licence as well and William Randall was a mill-wright. Drawn by Margaret Richardson

29

High Street, looking towards the church, from a mid-nineteenth-century sketch. Reproduced by Brian Drage from a photograph by Robert Ticehurst in the archives of the Marlow Society

The top of the High Street in the late nineteenth century showing Foottit's shop and London House. The dormer window of London House can still be seen in 1991 over Sketchley's shop. Reproduced by Brian Drage from a photograph by Robert Ticehurst in the archives of the Marlow Society

agency. It seems that Henry Salmon, an ironmonger who was also registrar of births, marriages and deaths, had the shop which later became Foottit's and that Emanuel Taylor, a draper and satin-stitch manufacturer from Birmingham, had the shop next door, shown as London House in illustrations and now occupied by Sketchley's. Incidentally Foottit's eventually became Snow's, and later Boots, an example of continuity of use for over a hundred years.

St Peter's Street

Relatively few well-to-do families lived in St Peter's Street. Thomas Gibbons was a coal merchant and farmer and was living at the top end of the street. He owned his house and garden, which was rated at £17, and rented an orchard from the Dean and Chapter of Gloucester. He also owned woodland at Spinfield and rented wharfage from the Alms House Trust. A man of sixty-four, he was born in Great Marlow; he lived with his wife Sarah, who came from Aylesbury, and his son William who worked as his father's assistant. On the night of the census they had a visitor, Mary Ann Wethered, the widow of Charles Wethered. John Morgan, the linen and woollen draper whose shop was in the High Street, lived nearby, probably in the house which was known as the Old Parsonage. His wife Eliza had been a Wright and so had inherited from Mary Wright's will. The Morgans rented their house from the Dean and Chapter of Gloucester and certainly the parsonage house was lived in by a Morgan at the time of the publication of the Victoria County History for Buckinghamshire in 1905. The house was built late in the fourteenth century; it was partly rebuilt in the seventeenth century and was extended more recently, but it still retains the original hall, the north and south walls of which each contain original fourteenth-century windows. The Morgan family, who were Dissenters like the Wrights, had two sons, Joseph Wright Morgan, probably named after his grandfather, and James William Morgan, both of whom worked as draper's assistants in their father's business.

General view of St Peter's Street c.1910. Photograph by H.W. Taunt, reproduced by courtesy of Buckinghamshire Museum

The Old Parsonage in 1991. Drawn by Margaret Richardson

Handkerchiefs bearing the initials of James William Morgan and his wife Fanny Havell Morgan (nee Wright) made for their wedding in 1861. The decoration is in satin stitch. Photograph by Brian Drage, reproduced by courtesy of Mrs Adams

The Weedon family lived in the Deanery, a separate house made out of part of the original parsonage house, which had acquired its name from that of James Deane, a former owner. Thomas Weedon was a paper manufacturer from Chesham, who had bought Temple

The north side of the Old Parsonage, showing one of the fourteenth-century traceried windows of the great hall. James Morgan, shown with his wife and daughter, built up the family firm. Reproduced by courtesy of Mrs Mary Adams

Mill from T.P.Williams in 1848. The family had only recently come to the town, probably from Rickmansworth in Hertfordshire since Mr Weedon's son and daughter were both born there. Mrs Weedon came from Hemel Hempstead; her unmarried sister also lived with the family and they had two house servants.

Tragedy hit the family in July 1851 as the following cutting from the *Windsor and Eton Express* for 2 August shows:

> **MAIDENHEAD.**
> FATAL GIG ACCIDENT.—An inquest was held at the Red Lion, Maidenhead, on Wednesday the 30th, ult.,before Rupert Clarke, Esq., on the body of Mr. William Arthur Weedon, of the Temple Paper Mills, near Great Marlow, aged 26 years, who met with a premature death in the following sudden and melancholy manner. The unfortunate deceased had been to town the previous day, and on returning from Maidenhead Station, about five o'clock, in his pony chaise to proceed home, when near the Chapel Arches, Maidenhead, from some cause one of the shafts became broken, and the pony endeavoured to kick, and ran away, when the deceased jumped out and fell backwards in the road ; the pony almost immediately afterwards ran against a carriage and broke the other shaft, and continued some distance with the shafts and steps. The deceased was picked up insensible and removed to the above house, where he was attended by Mr. Cridland (who saw the accident from his window), Mr. Goolden, and by the deceased's medical attendant, Mr. Wilkinson, of Marlow, who conjointly rendered every assistance, but without avail, as the deceased remained in a state of unconsciousness until a quarter before ten o'clock the same evening, when death took place, from a fracture of the base of the skull. Verdict—Accidental Death.

Mr Wilkinson, mentioned above as Mr Weedon's medical attendant, was living in High Street at the time.

The Roman Catholic church in St Peter's Street was completed in 1846. The land had been bought by Mr Scott Murray of Danesfield, Medmenham, and he also paid for the building of the church which was designed by Pugin. This was a time of strong anti-Catholic feeling, as can be seen from the following newspaper cutting from the *Windsor and Eton Express* of 10 January 1852:

CARDINAL WISEMAN has been staying at Danesfield, the seat of Mr Scott Murray, who may be recollected as one of the earlier "perverts" to the Romish faith. His eminence gave an address to the Roman Catholics of this town at the chapel on Tuesday evening, the subject being the "cardinal virtue" of humility, but it did not commend itself much by the example of this arrogant prelate as manifested by his aggressive policy.

The Roman Catholic church, built in 1846, by A.W. Pugin. Photograph by Peter Diplock, 1991

Apparently Murray did not disclose his reasons for acquiring the land until after the purchase. Recent additions have enlarged the original church which had one hundred seats. The records for 1851 show that there were sixteen baptisms and thirty-three confirmations; the parish at that time was extensive and included both High Wycombe and Maidenhead.

The Scott Murray family were not ostracised as a result of their support for the Catholic faith. Both Mr Scott Murray's wife and his mother were patronesses of the Ball held at the Town Hall on Thursday 15 January 1852. Advance notice appeared in the *Windsor and Eton Express* on 17 December 1851:

Ball, Marlow.

THERE will be a BALL at the TOWN HALL, MARLOW, on THURSDAY, January 15th, 1852, at Ten o'clock.

Ladies Patronesses.

THE RIGHT HONOURABLE THE COUNTESS OF ORKNEY.
THE RIGHT HONOURABLE LADY CAMOYS.
THE HONOURABLE MRS. SCOTT MURRAY.
MRS. BISHOP CULPEPER.
MRS. SCOTT MURRAY.
MRS. VANSITTART.
MRS. LANE.
MRS. OWEN WETHERED.

Tickets, including Refreshments, Eight Shillings each, may be had at Mr. Cannon's Library, and at the Crown Hotel.
Weippert's celebrated Band will attend. It will be a Moonlight night

The Reverend John Morris, priest at St Peter's Church, lived in the presbytery in St Peter's Street. He was only twenty-four and had been born in the East Indies; he had a housekeeper, Mrs June Rose, to look after him. The organist, Thomas Teal, was his neighbour. He was thirty-four and he too had a housekeeper, Mrs Sarah Jenner, whose eleven-year-old son Robert is also recorded in the census returns as a house servant.

Further down St Peter's Street, probably on the west side on the corner with Church Passage, lived Richard Gibbons, who was the town's other brewer. He was probably the younger brother of Thomas, the coal merchant, and John, the grocer and wine merchant in West Street. His two elder sons were in their father's business as brewer's assistants but Alfred, the youngest son, is described as a wine merchant's assistant and may have been working elsewhere, perhaps for his uncle. Mrs Gibbons and two daughters completed the family and they had a sixteen-year-old house servant.

In contrast the rest of the street housed several coal porters, who may have worked for Thomas Gibbons, and at least twelve agricultural labourers. Labourers from the paper mills lived there and at least four men worked in rope-making. There were three bargemen and two barge carters as well as wharfingers, men who owned or managed wharves; these are all occupations reflecting the nature of the river traffic at the time. Most wives had no stated occupation, but some women were employed as satin-stitch workers. Several daughters were given as servants, presumably working elsewhere by day and returning home at night. There were also dressmakers, laundresses and women who worked in the paper mill as rag sorters or rag cutters. Most of the houses in St Peter's

The Old Malt House, late eighteenth century. Richard Gibbons and his family almost certainly lived here in 1851. Photograph by Peter Diplock, 1991

Street were lived in by a single family, though there were at least two houses which were shared. Property ownership was well distributed amongst a large number of individual owners but only a few men lived in houses which they owned. Rents were relatively low; a whole row of small houses without gardens were each assessed at £3 for the year.

The ale-houses in the street were the Two Brewers, a Wethered house kept by Elizabeth Hobbs, and The Waterman, a Gibbons house, kept by Henry Neighbour. Both these houses had several lodgers and Elizabeth Hobbs, who had taken over the running of the Two Brewers after the death of her husband Samuel, had a general servant to help her. Samuel may have been related to John Hobbs, already mentioned as running the George and Dragon in The Causeway.

In 1851 the census returns record families whose address was 'the churchyard' or Church Passage. John Larkin, a journeyman carpenter aged thirty-four, lived in the churchyard with his wife and three small children as did John Johnson, a labourer at the paper mill, and William West, who also worked at the paper mill. Both Mr West and Mr Johnson had previously lived in Rickmansworth, according to the birthplace of their children, and may well have come to Marlow to work in the Weedon paper mill. The families in Church Passage included Maria Abbie, who said that she was the wife of a paper maker. Her husband is not recorded so was

The two sides of the inn sign at the Two Brewers. One side shows Thomas Wethered (1791-1849), the founder of Marlow's brewery, and the other Samuel Whitbread (1758-1815), founder of the firm which now owns the brewery. Photographs by Peter Diplock, 1991

St Peter's Street looking north, showing the Two Brewers. Photograph by H.W. Taunt, reproduced by courtesy of Buckinghamshire County Museum

presumably away on census night, but their three children are listed. Two of them were also born in Rickmansworth, including the one-year-old, so it is possible that this family had also moved to Marlow for work reasons. William Sparks was a victualler and lived with his wife and three children. He seems to have been a beer seller, according to the directories, but he had three lodgers at the time of the census and shared his house with another family. William Truss, sexton and shoemaker, was a neighbour; he was a widower and lived with his two daughters and his son. He also had a lodger, John Mossenden, another widower aged eighty-six who had been a shoemaker in his time. Two other families lived in Church Passage: John Brown, whose occupation looks like coal porter, and his wife, his brother-in-law and his sister-in-law, whose surname is Sparks, and three lodgers; and Frances Badger, mistress of the infant school. Jane Truss, aged eleven, is recorded as a visitor in her house; perhaps she was also one of William Truss's daughters and was acting as servant to Miss Badger.

None of these properties is still here today. Most of them were pulled down before the end of the nineteenth century and Church Passage is now no more than a footpath. But one can imagine the small houses, very near to the river, possibly subject to flooding and certainly damp. William Sparks probably provided the only opportunity for warmth and a gossip in his beer-house.

St Peter's Street in flood, early twentieth century. Reproduced by Brian Drage from a photograph by Robert Ticehurst in the archives of the Marlow Society

Spittal Street

The Crown Hotel, in Market Place at the top of the High Street, was run by Thomas Furnell in 1851 and more is written about this in the section on Inns, Ale-houses and Beer Sellers. To the east lies Spittal Street, which may take its name from the hospice or hospital of St Thomas, known to have been in existence in Marlow in 1384. In

The top of the High Street at the turn of the century, looking towards The Crown Hotel. Lovegrove's shop, seen on the right, is occupied by Oddbins in 1991. Photograph by H.W. Taunt, reproduced by courtesy of Buckinghamshire County Museum

1851 the street contained one of the town's inns, The Greyhound, which was owned by Wethered, and an ale-house called The Cross Keys, owned by T.P.Williams. There were also two beer sellers.

In general the street contained respectable craftsmen and retailers. This is well demonstrated by looking at the south side of Spittal Street, from the top of the High Street to The Cross Keys. The first two houses were owned by T.P.Williams, as was a good deal of the property in the street; some of the houses featured in the sale of the Williams estate in 1905 and the details provide useful corroboration for the attempted repopulation. The house next to Number 1 High Street was empty at the time of the census. It was included in the sale, when it was described as a freehold shop and house of three floors, with a yard containing kitchen, scullery, offices, sheds and a large warehouse. At the time it was let to George Dorsett, who was a grocer. The house next door, now Jasmine Peking, was lived in by William Westbrook in 1851. He

37

Oddbins shop in 1991.
Drawn by Margaret
Richardson

George Dorsett's shop,
empty in 1851. Reproduced
by Brian Drage from a
photograph by Robert
Ticehurst in the archives of
the Marlow Society

was a master butcher, who had a journeyman butcher working for him, together with an apprentice and an errand boy, all of whom lived in the house. Mr Westbrook was a widower and had one house servant. His house is described in the sale details as a freehold butcher's shop and house, with three bedrooms on each of the top two floors. The description continues:

There is an Excellent Timber and Tiled Barn, converted into Six-Stall Stable, Loose Boxes and Slaughter-house, and these front on to the private thoroughfare leading out of Spittal Street. Further down this thoroughfare are an Open Shed, a Strip of Garden Ground and Useful Meadow, in which have been erected by the Tenant several Pigstyes and Sheds.

Obviously the premises had remained as a butcher's shop for over fifty years and the timber barn is still visible today.

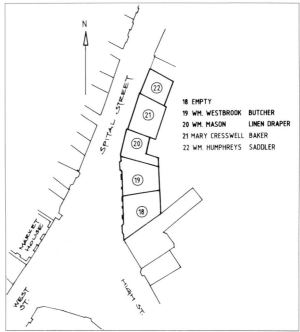

18 EMPTY
19 WM. WESTBROOK   BUTCHER
20 WM. MASON   LINEN DRAPER
21 MARY CRESSWELL   BAKER
22 WM. HUMPHREYS   SADDLER

Next to Westbrook lived William Mason, a linen draper, with his wife, a milliner, and their two young children. William's brother lived there also, and seems to have been apprenticed to his older brother, and the household was completed by a servant.

The Masons' neighbours were Creswells, a familiar Marlow name at the time. Mary Creswell, an eighty-year-old widow, lived there with her married daughter, a laundress, and her three daughters. Also in the house were John Creswell and his wife and their four children. John was a baker and it looks as if his father was before him; his mother's occupation is given as 'formerly baker'. Still in the same house, according to the census returns, were James Cox and his wife. He is recorded as a farmer of thirty-five acres, employing three labourers, and he features in the directory as a cow keeper. This house is described in the sale details as being a freehold shop and house on two floors. The shop front had been modernised by 1905, but reference is made to the yard at the rear with timber and tiled outhouses and the fact that the property had access to part of the barn.

Next to the Creswell household was William Humphreys, a saddler employing two men. As well as his family, an annuitant, William Gregory, lived in the house. Gregory was one of the census enumerators, covering the west side of the High Street, West Street and other streets

Timber-framed barn in Morris Place off Spittal Street, recently renovated. Photograph by Bill Purser, 1991

in that part of the town. William Crouch lived next door in a house owned by Williams. He was a farmer of twelve acres, employing two labourers. A widower, Mr Crouch lived with his son who helped with the farm, and they had a house servant. This was another two-storey house and was let to an ironmonger at the time of the sale in 1905.

The next three houses were owned by the parish and housed an agricultural labourer and his family, a sawyer with his wife and son, who was an apprentice cordwainer, and a carpenter's labourer.

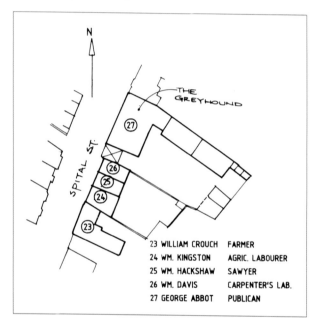

23	WILLIAM CROUCH	FARMER
24	WM. KINGSTON	AGRIC. LABOURER
25	WM. HACKSHAW	SAWYER
26	WM. DAVIS	CARPENTER'S LAB.
27	GEORGE ABBOT	PUBLICAN

George Abbot ran The Greyhound. He was a man of forty from Streatley in Berkshire. He and his wife had three children of whom only the youngest, a two-year-old boy, had been born in Great Marlow, suggesting that the family had only recently come to the town. The inn had been run by Henry Wyatt in 1842, but later directories show that George continued as landlord for the next few years and that he had been succeeded by his wife by 1864. He had living-in help in Thomas Collins, a local man, who was an ostler. Several of the town's carrier services ran from The Greyhound.

Between The Greyhound and The Cross Keys lived Richard Davis, butcher, Joseph Eagle, grocer, Thomas Wigginton, coal merchant, William East, butcher, Thomas Mitchell, agricultural labourer, William Wyatt, cabinet-maker, and Samuel Smith, maltster. The Cross Keys was run by Henry Thomas Meakes, who was one of another familiar Marlow family. Meakes was also a smith and probably the son of Joshua Meakes, a shoeing smith, who lived on the other side of the street.

The north side of Spittal Street shows a similar mix. Thomas Walker was a furniture broker, living next to the Crown. His neighbours were William Reeves, journeyman carpenter and joiner, and Francis Allum, fishmonger. James Creswell, master butcher, lived on this side of the street. In all there were four butchers in Spittal Street and it is tempting to think that perhaps this part of the town had traditionally been the area for this trade. But closer study suggests that there were butchers' shops in most of the main streets of the town. Although there is an abbatoir at the bottom of Dukes Place it is known that earlier this century each butcher did his own slaughtering at the back of his premises. The census returns suggest that butchers

The Cross Keys in 1991. Photograph by Bill Purser

41

were well-to-do, in that all four households included servants or housekeepers.

A significant number of the craftsmen are recorded as journeymen, showing that they had completed their apprenticeship. These included four carpenters, a wheelwright, a shoemaker and a cooper. There was also a master plumber, employing both a journeyman plumber and an apprentice. Joshua Meakes's smithy was a Williams property and is described in the sale details as a freehold smithy, workshops and two cottages. The whole provided 'excellent accommodation for the trade of a Blacksmith'.

Chapel Street

The Primitive Methodist Chapel, Liston Hall, was not built until 1874 but the street was called Chapel Street in the Census Returns. Langley (1797) says that the name comes from an earlier chapel in Marlow called The Hermitage. The Reverend Thomas Styles, Independent Minister, who lived in Chapel Street, was the minister of the Salem Chapel in Quoiting Place. Mr Styles, who was

General view of Chapel Street, early twentieth century. Barnard's Stores appears in this street as well as in Spittal Street. Reproduced from a post-card

fifty-five at the time of the census, had a servant to look after him; he had been in Marlow for over ten years and was a bachelor. It seems that he then decided to marry and caused some concern amongst some of the members of his church because the lady in question was his cook. The tale is told in the history of the chapel and the letter, signed by William Gregory and Joseph Wright and stating that the alliance was 'imprudent and disreputable', is quoted in full. The future Mrs Styles does not seem to have been in the household on census night; apart from the minister himself only his house servant, aged sixty, and a female visitor, aged thirty, are recorded. In any event the marriage went ahead and Mr Styles remained in office until 1863.

Benjamin Atkinson, listed among the gentry in the directories, lived at The Rookery; his initials can still be seen on the outside wall of what was the stable block. He does not appear in the census returns so was presumably away at the time, but his butler and housekeeper are recorded. Mr Atkinson owned quite a lot of property in Marlow, some of it in Chapel Street. Thomas Matthews was running a boarding school at Prospect House which was at the east end of Chapel Street at the junction of the Wycombe and Little Marlow roads. Later the house on this site was called The Swallows; there is no evidence that it was the same building as the one which housed the school and it has now been demolished. The census returns record eleven resident scholars at Prospect House.

Atkinson initials. Photographs by Peter Diplock, 1991

General view of Rookery Lodge in 1991. Drawn by Margaret Richardson

Thomas Matthews was twenty-nine and his wife Caroline was thirty; they had a four-year old son and two servants.

Nearby lived John Meadows from Lincoln, a proprietor of houses. He was also listed among the gentry, presumably because he was a man of property. His wife Elizabeth was almost twenty years older than he was and her sister, an annuitant, lived with them. It is tempting to speculate that Mr Meadows married his wife for her money, which enabled him to develop his interests in property. The household was completed by one servant. Very few households in Chapel Street included servants. Apart from those already mentioned, Mr Wellicome, a grocer, had a fourteen-year-old servant, Ann Frith. Ann, who was born in Great Marlow, may have been the oldest daughter of William and Sarah Frith, who also lived in Chapel Street, but it has not been possible to trace this in the register of births. William was a bricklayer's labourer and the family consisted of six children. Mrs Abear, a widow of ninety-two who was an annuitant, lived with her daughter, also an annuitant, and a house servant of thirteen.

The ale-houses in Chapel Street were The Horns, a Wethered house kept by George Wyatt, who was also a carrier, and The White Hart, owned by T.P.Williams and run by William Plumridge. Three beer sellers are listed. They were William Chilton, who was also a marine store dealer; George Finch, who was a brewer's drayman; and Diana Smith, a widow of forty with seven children, aged between one and thirteen. William Chilton's house was owned by Mrs Pym, but Finch's house was owned by Clayton, which suggests that he was working for Gibbons rather than for Wethered. Richard Gibbons was a supporter of Sir William Clayton, Whig, and it is unlikely that a Wethered employee would be living in a Clayton house. Mrs Smith lived in a Williams house, valued at £13; not only did she have a visitor on census night, Joseph Porter who was a journeyman cordwainer from Wokingham, but she shared the house with another Marlow family consisting of James Hawes, paper maker, his wife and their three children. So this house contained four adults and ten children at the time of the census.

Over twenty men were recorded as shoemakers or cordwainers and twelve as agricultural labourers. Other occupations included carpenter, blacksmith, gardener, bricklayer and painter, while several men were labourers at the brewery. It is possible to trace one or two men from Wethered wage lists; William Nichols, who lived with his wife and unmarried daughter, was a storehouseman earning fifteen shillings a week in 1858 and Daniel Lovegrove was town drayman who earned twelve shillings a week at the same period. Daniel's son George also appears on the wages sheet as a labourer at the brewery. Henry Stallwood, who was Returning Officer and Bailiff for the County Court, was also collector of the Poor Rates. He was one of the census enumerators and covered part of the outlying area of the parish, including the old workhouse. George Painter, the Relieving Officer, also lived in Chapel Street. He does not appear in the census but is included in the Rate Book.

The most common occupation recorded for women was satin-stitch work, followed by dressmaking and lace making. Interestingly, two women are recorded as being 'on the parish', one as being 'on parish relief' and one as being a pauper.

The distribution of people recorded in some way in the census returns as paupers is interesting and sometimes surprising. The table overleaf gives the details for census groups 1,2 and 3.

The surprising feature is that paupers are by no means restricted to the poorer parts of the town. It is true that there are none recorded for High Street but there are eight entries for West Street and four for Chapel Street in marked contrast to the three recorded for Dean Street. In the case of the younger people listed it is not clear whether they are still working. The two teenage men are something of a mystery; perhaps they were not capable of employment. In some cases it seems likely that families were being paid to house and feed an elderly pauper, not always a member of the family.

Dean Street

The picture of this street which is provided by the census returns and other sources suggests that it differs from the other streets which have been studied in one or

Name	Age	Address and other details, including how described
Sarah Barnes	66	Chapel Street: widow living with daughter and granddaughter. On the parish.
Joseph Birch	73	West Street: living with wife. Pauper, no previous occupation given.
John Brown	72	West Street: living with wife, daughter and granddaughter. Pauper/gardener.
Rebecca Camden	48	West Street: widow living with two sons and two daughters. Pauper/lace maker.
Ann East	75	Spittal Street: widow living with granddaughter. Pauper, formerly umbrella maker.
Richard East	77	Dean Street: widower living alone. Pauper/agricultural labourer.
J.Eaton	18	West Street: male living with mother, brother and sister. Beggar.
M.Fisher	77	West Street: single female living with a family. Pauper/lace maker.
Elisabeth Frith	47	Gun Lane: widow living with daughter, son-in-law and their child. Pauper, formerly lace maker.
John Frith	52	West Street: living with wife and sister. Pauper/labourer.
Elizabeth Harris	88	Chapel Street: widow living with son and family. On parish relief.
J.Holmes	72	West Street: widower living as a lodger. Pauper/labourer.
Ann Hopkins	82	Gun Lane: widow living with daughter, son-in-law and their two children. Pauper, formerly lace maker.
William James	72	West Street: widower living with daughter. Pauper, no previous occupation given.
Ellen Leary	46	St.Peter's Street: widow living with two sons. Poor woman.
Mary Loftin	87	Quoiting Place: widow living with daughter. Pauper, formerly lace maker.
Mary Pimm	52	Marefield: single, sharing house with married couple. Pauper/seamstress.
Ann Smith	64	Oxford Terrace: widow living with granddaughter and grandson. Pauper/cook.
Elizabeth Smith	77	Chapel Street: widow living with son, daughter-in-law and family and daughter. Pauper, formerly lace maker.
Mary Stevens	55	Dean Street: single living with two other families. Pauper/lace maker.
Martha White	80	Chapel Street: widow living with nephew and his family. On the parish.
William White	16	Dean Street: living with mother and brother. Pauper. Note: lives in same house as Mary Stevens.

General view of Dean Street, probably c.1910. Dean Street used to be known as The City because it contained ale-houses called The Mint, The Royal Exchange and The Bank of England. Reproduced by Brian Drage

'The Bank of England', probably c.1910. Reproduced by Brian Drage from a photograph owned by Mrs Price, whose husband's family were licensees from the late nineteenth century.

two significant ways. For one thing, the houses, judging by their rateable value, are smaller – by far the majority of them are valued at under £5 – and many of them do not have gardens. Secondly. the number of people living in these small houses is often large, sometimes consisting of two parents and up to eight children but also, on occasion, involving multi-occupancy of the house by two or more families. Here are two examples:

George Anderson	head	32	**agricultural labourer**
Emma	wife	28	
Reuben	son	6	scholar
Mary	daughter	1	
share a house with			
Sarah Green	widow	35	satin-stitch worker
Alexander	son	14	
Alice	daughter	8	
Thomas	son	6	
Thomas Grove	visitor	20	**agricultural labourer**
Joseph East jnr.	head	29	gardener
Eliza	wife	26	
James	son	2	scholar
Rachel	daughter	8 mns.	
share a house with			
Absalom Allum	lodger	27	fishmonger
Sarah	wife	24	
Jane	daughter	6 mns.	

All these individuals were born in the county and all except George Anderson and Absalom Allum in Great Marlow. This is true of most of the inhabitants of Dean Street and the overall impression is of a closely-knit and local community, with several surnames recurring many times such as Price, Bowles, Stroud and Harris. The names in the Rate Book follow those in the census returns very closely, suggesting that families remained in the same house for several years. Joseph East, for instance, is referred to as 'junior' and his father, also Joseph and also a gardener, lived in Dean Street also. There were several Allum families in the town and Absalom was in all probability the son of Francis Allum, also a fishmonger, who had his house and shop in Market Street close to the Crown Hotel; Absalom almost certainly worked there, as did his younger brother who still lived at home.

Property in Dean Street was owned by a variety of

people. Clayton and Williams feature as might be expected, but Ralph Harris, who lived in West Street, owned twenty houses, and William Creswell, coal merchant and farmer, owned twelve. Only four men in the entire street owned the house in which they lived; they were William Wigginton, who also owned five other properties, James Bowles, who owned two houses and lived in one of them, Jeremiah Humphrey who kept a lodging-house and Richard Hayes, whose wife, Grace, was the mistress of the infant school in Dean Street.

An analysis of the occupations of the men is shown in the following table:

Occupation	Number	Percentage of total
Agricultural labourer	110	54.18
Shoemaker	17	8.37
Bricklayer	13	6.40
Fruiterer	12	5.91
Skewer maker	7	3.44
Beer seller	7	3.44
Gardener	4	1.97
Baker	3	1.47
Bargeman	3	1.47
Lodging-house keeper	3	1.47
Tobacco pipe maker	3	1.47
Brick maker	2	0.98
Carpenter	2	0.98
Chimney sweep	2	0.98
Grocer	2	0.98
Tailor	2	0.98
Butcher	1	0.49
Letter carrier	1	0.49
Millwright	1	0.49
Veterinary surgeon	1	0.49
Fishmonger	1	0.49
Gas stoker	1	0.49
Mason's labourer	1	0.49
Plasterer	1	0.49
Sawyer	1	0.49
Paper maker	1	0.49
Hurdle maker	1	0.49
Groom	1	0.49
Coal porter	1	0.49
Blacksmith's labourer	1	0.49
Wood hewer	1	0.49
Servant	1	0.49

The overwhelming number of agricultural labourers living in Dean Street suggests that this was one of the less-well-off areas although, as we have seen, only three paupers were recorded for the street. It is noticeable that there are fewer tradesmen and craftsmen and far more unskilled workers. The shoemakers are the next largest group and a more detailed look will show the range of skill which was represented.

Richard Carr was a master shoemaker, employing two boys; these were his two sons, aged 15 and 12 and living at home.

Daniel Pert was a master shoemaker, employing a journeyman of 16, who was his wife's son, presumably by a former marriage, and another shoemaker, his nephew, aged 21.

Seven other men said that they were journeymen, implying that they had finished their apprenticeship. The youngest of these was 17 so both he and Daniel Pert's assistant must have been apprenticed at an early age.

Those who are described as apprentices are aged eleven, thirteen, fifteen and eighteen.

There are three other men whose occupation is given as shoemaker, without further qualification.

The bricklayers' group similarly includes two bricklayers, two apprentices and nine bricklayer's labourers.

Some of the workers were very young. The youngest agricultural labourer was eleven and there were also ten errand boys, ranging in age from nine to sixteen. One of the skewer makers, James Langley, was also only eleven and he, together with James Perry aged nineteen, another skewer maker, was brought before the Quarter Sessions in 1851 charged with 'damaging trees growing'.

There are three lodging-house keepers listed for Dean Street. William Price had ten lodgers on census night as well as a second family of two in his house, which he rented from Sir William Clayton and which must have been one of the largest in the street for the rateable value was given as £13. Jeremiah Humphrey had thirteen lodgers in a house which was also valued at £13 and which the Rate Book indicates that he had inherited. George Carr's property was smaller, valued at £6, and he had six lodgers. He rented the house from the executors of the late A.Webb. Apart from these acknowledged lodging-houses many of the other households in Dean Street also included lodgers, listed as such in the census returns. It is also tempting to wonder whether all the people listed as visitors were only temporary residents or whether some of these were lodgers too.

All three lodging-house keepers were also beer sellers, as were four other Dean Street men, each of whom had another occupation as well. George Clarke and Samuel Beckett were both journeymen carpenters, William Croxon was a bargeman and William Brown may also have been a boot and shoemaker, according to directories. In the census return he is described as a victualler and was running the Jolly Maltsters, a property owned by T.P.Williams.

Many of the women of Dean Street also worked, particularly daughters living at home. The details are given in the following table:

Satin-stitch worker	**51**
Lace maker	**31**
Rag sorter	**13**
Seamstress	**9**
Rag cutter	**7**
Servant	**7**
Laundress	**6**
Dressmaker	**5**
Embroideress	**2**
Fancy needle worker	**2**
Charwoman	**2**
Paper sorter	**1**
Shoe binder	**1**
Schoolmistress	**1**

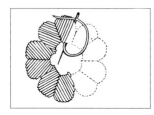

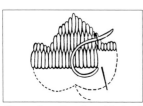

Examples of various kinds of satin stitch, taken from *Dictionary of Stitches*, 1934, by Mary Thomas

Some of these working women were also very young; one satin-stitch worker was twelve, a rag sorter was thirteen and a seamstress was fifteen. The assistant schoolmistress was only sixteen. It is worth pointing out that of the seven servants only two were servants to Dean Street households. One of these was Harriet Smith, who was a servant in the household of James Frewing, millwright, and his wife Elizabeth. The Frewings had three children, aged eleven, nine and seven, all of whom were described as scholars. The other servant was Hannah Bowers, in the household of William Wigginton, grocer, who lived in his own house with his wife and their five children, aged between ten years and eleven months.

Attempts to repopulate the street were not very successful. Essentially this is because the houses shown on the 1876 map are nearly all small, without any real distinguishing features, and almost all of them have since been pulled down. Because the rateable values are low and often very similar it is not easy to be sure who lived where. In practice this is not important; the detailed information which the census returns provide is enough to give the feel of the area and so we have not included any repopulation maps for Dean Street. But it is worth mentioning that about one-fifth of the entire population of the parish lived here. In 1851 it was felt that the Parish Church was inadequate to look after all these people on its own and in February the Incorporated Society for Promoting the Enlargement and Building of Churches agreed to a grant for the building of a new church for 'the large number of poor persons'. It was reported in the *Bucks Herald* that the parish church 'is occupied almost exclusively by the wealthier classes, there being but 32 free seats for adults out of 1200 and 238 for the children of the poor'.

The Reverend Frederick Bussell petitioned the Bishop to consecrate the new church, which had been built on land owned by T.P.Williams and which he had sold for the purpose. The plan is drawn in the margin of the Bishop's reply and shows that the site was in Gun Lane as it then was, bounded on the east by the Three Horse Shoes ale-house and its garden, on the north by the path from Marlow Field to Dean Street, on the south by Gun Lane and on the west by property belonging to Williams

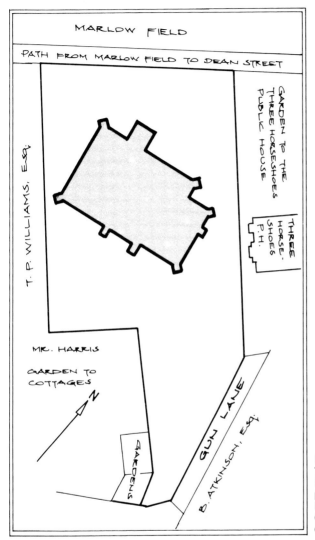

MARLOW FIELD

PATH FROM MARLOW FIELD TO DEAN STREET

T. P. WILLIAMS, ESQ.

GARDEN TO THE THREE HORSESHOES PUBLIC HOUSE

THREE HORSE-SHOES P.H.

MR. HARRIS

GARDEN TO COTTAGES

N

GARDENS

GUN LANE

B. ATKINSON, ESQ.

Plan of the site of Holy Trinity Church from the Bishop's reply to the original petition. Drawn by Joan Rogers after the original in Oxfordshire County Record Office

and to Ralph Harris. One of the previous buildings on the site was known as the Garrison and had presumably housed soldiers at one time, giving rise to the name of Gun Lane. It had been pulled down as a 'slum clearance', having been in multi-occupancy certainly since 1841, according to the census returns for that year. The new church was dedicated to the Holy Trinity and contained five hundred free and open sittings. It served as a chapel of ease to the parish church, which meant that it could carry out all religious ceremonies except the celebration of marriage and the burial of the dead. Gun Lane changed its name to Trinity Lane as a result.

West Street

In many ways West Street resembled High Street. It contained a wide range of houses, varying in value from the £100 accorded to Remnantz, the home of the Wethered family, to the £3 and £3 10s. values so common in Dean Street. Characteristically, or so it seems, few men lived in houses which they owned, though they might well own property elsewhere. Actual ownership is shown in the following table:

Sir William Clayton	43	
T.P.Williams	33	
Ralph Harris	14	including his own house
Robert Hammond	6	including his own house
Wethered family	6	including Remnantz
Feoffees of the Free School	4	
Dean & Chapter, Bristol	3	
Francis Hone	3	
James Beckett	2	including his own house
Thomas Corby	2	
Rachel Hall	2	
Mrs Lovegrove	2	
George Wyatt	2	
Henry Badger	1	
Brakspear	1	
R.E.Edwards	1	
John Gibbons	1	his own house
William Grant	1	
Thomas Hickman	1	his own house
James Lovegrove	1	his own house
Marlow Parish	1	
Margaret Morris	1	
Richard Smith	1	his own house
Neville Reid & Co.	1	
Elizabeth Ward	1	the family house

General view of West Street in the 1920s. Reproduced by Brian Drage from a photograph by Robert Ticehurst in the archives of the Marlow Society

As already mentioned, Remnantz was the home of the Wethered family. In 1851 Mrs Sarah Wethered lived there with her son Lawrence. The house was described as a mansion and the rest of the property consisted of a pleasure ground, summerhouses, a greenhouse and a garden. In addition the Rate Book records that the Wethereds occupied an adjacent house, owned by their neighbour Robert Hammond and later known as The Heathers, so called because Mr Heather, schoolmaster of the Free School, once lived there. It was apparently not in use at the time of the census. Two Wethered daughters were at home, Martha and Anne, and the census returns

Remnantz in 1991, still the Wethered family home. Drawn by Margaret Richardson

55

record six servants: footman, groom, cook, lady's maid, housemaid and kitchen maid.

The footman, J.Stockbridge, was a married man and it looks as if his wife Sarah lived in a Wethered house nearby with the rest of the Stockbridge family – a daughter of seventeen and a son of thirteen both described as servants, who may possibly have worked at Remnantz during the day but continued to live at home, and two younger children who were said to be scholars.

Robert Hammond lived in Western House. He had been a lieutenant in the Royal Navy and was farming two hundred acres at Copy Green. A man of fifty, he had a wife of twenty-six and three living-in servants. It is likely that the men who lived in some of his other houses were also his employees; William Marcham, for example, was a

The staff of Remnantz outside the side door; exact date unknown. Reproduced by courtesy of Mrs G. Reeves

groom and Joseph Tilby and his two sons were all farm labourers.

Ralph Harris, who owned property in Dean Street, also owned the block of houses which made up the Gardens, sometimes called Harris's Gardens. He was a retired cabinet-maker aged sixty and lived in his own house in the Gardens with his wife, two sons and a daughter.

Other men who owned the houses in which they lived included James Beckett, a widower of sixty-five who lived in Quoiting Place. He was a master carpenter, employing four men and an apprentice, and might well have been the father – and employer, for that matter – of Henry Beckett, forty-two, who was also a carpenter and who also lived in Quoiting Place. Henry's house was owned by Clayton but Samuel Beckett, probably Henry's brother, lived in a house in Dean Street owned by James Beckett, who had quite a lot of property there. Samuel was also a carpenter and may also have worked for his father.

John Gibbons was a grocer and tallow chandler living quite near the Market Square end of West Street. He was sixty-six and employed three men. He lived with his wife, two sons, a daughter and one servant in what was probably a substantial house valued at £35. Thomas Hickman, timber merchant, also owned the house he lived in and so did James Lovegrove, a plumber who employed four men, an apprentice and a labourer. Richard Smith, a widower, was a shoemaker; he owned and lived in quite a small house, valued at £7.

It is probably already clear that the social mix in West Street was quite varied. This is born out by an analysis of the occupations. Farm labourers and shoemakers head the list, as they do in Dean Street, but they represent a much smaller percentage of the total. There was a wide range of traders and craftsmen, as well as farmers, schoolmasters, a china dealer, a medical dispenser and an Excise Officer. The first table lists those occupations followed by two or more men.

Initials on lead drain-pipe headers on Western House. Their identity is not known. Photographs by Peter Diplock, 1991

Western House. Photograph by Peter Diplock, 1991

Occupation	Number	Percentage of total
Farm labourer	30	16.75
Shoemaker	14	7.82
Labourer	11	6.14
Baker	10	5.58
Carpenter	10	5.58
Servant	7	3.91
Tailor	7	3.91
Blacksmith	6	3.35
Brewer's labourer	6	3.35
Gardener	6	3.35
Paper maker	5	2.79
Victualler	5	2.79
Groom	4	2.23
Bricklayer's labourer	3	1.67
Grocer	3	1.67
Harness maker	3	1.67
Plumber	3	1.67
Wheelwright	3	1.67
Basket maker	2	1.11
Brewer	2	1.11
Bricklayer	2	1.11
Butcher	2	1.11
Cabinet maker	2	1.11
Draper	2	1.11
Farm bailiff/steward	2	1.11
Farmer	2	1.11
Sawyer	2	1.11
Schoolmaster	2	1.11
Straw drawer	2	1.11

This accounts for almost 82% of the male occupations. The remaining 18% is made up of occupations followed by individuals and, again, the range is wide. Not suprisingly this is the group which includes craftsmen, like a plasterer; traders, such as a fishmonger; and professionals. It is worth setting out the list in full.

Beer retailer	Beggar (perhaps not an occupation)
Brazier	Carrier
Chimney sweep	China dealer
Coachman	Coal merchant
Confectioner	Engine driver
Excise officer	Fishmonger

Footman	Gamekeeper
Garden boy	Garden labourer
Machine maker	Medical dispenser
Mill labourer	Painter
Parish clerk	Plasterer
Postman	Postmaster
Printer/compositor	Rent collector
Rope maker	Saddler
Solicitor	Surgeon
Tea & coffee dealer	Timber merchant
Umbrella maker	Watch & clock maker

For women the range of occupations is much more restricted, but West Street contained two governesses, four schoolmistresses, a butcher, a milliner and a stationer as well as the expected laundresses, seamstresses, dressmakers and fancy needle workers.

Occupation	Number	Percentage of total
Servant	33	29.46
Laundress	15	13.39
Seamstress	11	9.82
Dressmaker	10	8.92
Fancy needle worker	10	8.92
Lace maker	7	6.25
Schoolmistress	4	3.57
Embroideress	3	2.67
Nurse	3	2.67
Cap maker	3	1.78
Governess	2	1.78
Paper mill worker	2	1.78

This accounts for just over 90% of the working women in West Street. The other 9% is made up of individuals and includes the butcher and the stationer, a straw-bonnet maker, a victualler and a solitary satin-stitch worker. It is interesting to compare these details with similar ones for Dean Street. The total number of working women was 112 in West Street and 129 in Dean Street. The following table shows comparative percentages for those occupations which turn up in both streets:

Occupation	West Street	Dean Street
Servant	29.46	5.42
Laundress	13.39	4.65
Seamstress	9.82	6.97
Dressmaker	8.92	3.87
Fancy needle worker	8.92	1.55
Lace maker	6.25	23.25
Schoolmistress	3.57	0.77
Embroideress	2.67	1.55
Satin-stitch worker	0.89	39.53

Some noticeable contrasts can be seen. Of the thirty-three servants in West Street most were living with the individual households by whom they were employed, whereas in Dean Street there were only two living-in servants. The major differences are in the numbers of satin-stitch workers and lace makers and there seems to be no obvious reason for this. Perhaps piece work of this kind was preferred by women of poorer households with larger families than, for example, the job of laundress which was the occupation of quite a lot of women in West Street.

Repopulating West Street was not always straightforward. The order of names in the census returns and in the Rate Book does not always agree and this makes it difficult to be sure who lived in a particular house. The clearest section is probably that on the south side of the street running from High Street as far as the Red Lion on the corner of Potlands.

William Wray and his wife, both in their late twenties, lived on the corner, in what was later to become Fryer's Dining Rooms. Mr Wray was a baker, once convicted at the Epiphany Quarter Sessions of 'using an unjust pair of scales', and the house was owned by T.P.Williams. When the Williams estate was sold in 1905 the property was described as 'splendid freehold premises' consisting of three rooms on the first floor and two on the second floor, with a shop, dining room and kitchen on the ground floor. The census returns record a Fryer family living in Dean Street in 1851. They had two young sons at the time, but it was not possible to find out whether Mrs S.J.Fryer, who held the lease for Fryer's

Dining Rooms at the time of the sale in 1905, had actually married one of them.

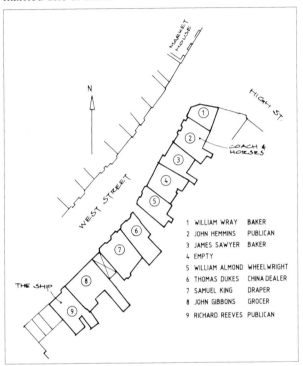

1 WILLIAM WRAY   BAKER
2 JOHN HEMMINS   PUBLICAN
3 JAMES SAWYER   BAKER
4 EMPTY
5 WILLIAM ALMOND   WHEELWRIGHT
6 THOMAS DUKES   CHINA DEALER
7 SAMUEL KING   DRAPER
8 JOHN GIBBONS   GROCER
9 RICHARD REEVES   PUBLICAN

Next door was the Coach and Horses. According to the census returns this was run by John Hemmins and his wife in 1851. They were not natives of the town and had probably not been there for long since their one-year-old daughter had been born in Egham. Nor did they stay for any length of time; in the Rate Book Hemmins' name is crossed out and that of Henry Pike is substituted and the directories give John Stephenson as the landlord in 1851 and Charles Haines in 1853. Their neighbours were the Sawyer family. James Sawyer, forty-eight, was a baker from Marlow and lived with his wife, their daughter of seventeen who was a dressmaker, and four sons aged between three and fifteen. They had one servant. This pattern of respectable craftsman or trader families, with one or sometimes two servants, was repeated down the street. William Almond, from West Wycombe, was a

61

wheelwright, Thomas Dukes, from Aylesbury, was a china dealer, Samuel King, also from Aylesbury, was a draper and John Gibbons, a Marlow man, was a grocer. Mr Dukes had established himself in Marlow by 1842 and continued to live in the town until his death in 1893 at the age of eighty-one. During his long life he was a lay preacher and class leader at the Methodist Church. He continued to run his shop until he was at least seventy and after his death the family business was continued by John Dennis Dukes. The property was let to a Miss Dukes, glass merchant, who was probably Thomas's eldest daughter, at the time of the sale of the Williams estate and is described as a 'freehold double-fronted shop and house'. It consisted of the shop with a sitting room, kitchen and offices behind, four bedrooms on the first floor and an attic.

Next to the Gibbons House was the Ship Inn, owned by T.P.Williams and run by Richard Reeves and his wife. This building also features in the 1905 sale and is described as:

The valuable
Freehold Fully-licensed Public House
known as
"The Ship", West Street,
being an attractive half-timbered property with ample
accommodation
for doing a good trade

It consisted of a sitting room, parlour, public bar, kitchen and excellent cellars, with four rooms upstairs. There was a garden with a skittle alley, a small stable, a coal cellar and offices.

Nearby was a substantial house valued at £30, owned by Wethered and occupied by Mrs Rose Frew, who was not there on the night of the census, her children, her sister and two servants. Next door but one was James Hunt, a tailor employing two men; he came from Lancashire and his wife was born in Nottingham. The family had been in Marlow for some time since their six sons, aged between twelve years and nine months, had all been born in the town. They had one servant. Henry Curtis, a surgeon from Dorking, together with his groom and house servant, lived next door to Thomas Hickman, a timber merchant. Hickman lived with his wife and daughter, two nephews and a niece; he came from Crowmarsh but his wife and the rest of the household were all born in Marlow.

Two or three doors down was Rachel Hall, a widow described as a butcher. Mrs Hall owned property in Marlow, including her own house which she shared with members of her own family, a lodger, one or more visitors and a servant. Nearby lived William Tyler, described as postmaster and agent. He was fifty-five, from Haddenham, and lived with his wife and unmarried sister-in-law, both Marlow women, and his mother-in-law who came from Abingdon. Caroline Anthony, stationer and a widow, lived next door in one of Robert Hammond's houses and next to her was Richard Smith, living in his own house.

The Red Lion was owned by Wethered and was run by Thomas Bowen, who was also the town's Surveyor of the Highways. Bowen was a man of fifty-one from Marlow. His household on census night included his wife, aged thirty-eight, who came from Bampton, a 'daughter-in-law' of sixteen, presumably his wife's child, a married sister, a seventeen-year-old labourer, and a female visitor aged seventeen from Reading.

Mention has already been made of James and Henry Beckett, both of whom lived in Quoiting Square. Henry Badger, the parish clerk, also lived here. He was a Marlow man and was forty-three at the time of the census. His wife, who was a schoolmistress, was forty-four and came from Medmenham. They had a daughter of eight who was a scholar and a son of seventeen who was an apprentice cabinet maker. Mrs Badger's mother lived with them and they had a thirteen-year-old servant. The Badgers' house was owned by T.P.Williams, as was the house, shop and

Inn sign from The Red Lion. Photograph by Peter Diplock, 1991

Quoiting Square, with the Clayton Arms on the right. The arch to the yard was later raised to allow the passage of loaded chair-wagons. Reproduced by courtesy of Buckinghamshire County Museum

64

yard rented by John Blackwell, a smith employing seven men. He came from Medmenham and lived with his wife, four sons between the ages of fifteen and three months and a two-year old daughter. All the children were born in Marlow and the family had a fifteen-year-old servant. This property was included in the 1905 sale and was described as a freehold house, smithy and cottage on the east side of Oxford Road. The house consisted of front room, kitchen, larder and cellar, with three good bedrooms and usual offices. There was a large smithy with four forges and also a freehold cottage. The property was still let to a Mr Blackwell, presumably one of the sons recorded in the census returns.

Benjamin Stallwood was another resident of Quoiting Square, probably living next door to the Clayton Arms. His house was owned by Clayton and Mr Stallwood was a printer and compositor. Neither he nor his wife came from Marlow, but their large family of four daughters and three sons, aged between fifteen and one, had all been born in the town. According to the directories the ale-house was run by Joseph Tyler in 1851, but the census returns state that it is his widow, Elizabeth Tyler, who is the victualler. Mrs Tyler was forty-five and came from Marlow. Her household included her married daughter Ann Moss, her son-in-law Henry Moss, a three-year-old granddaughter and a lodger. Whether Joseph Tyler had been of the same family as William Tyler is not known.

West Street had another ale-house in 1851, the Three Tuns, owned by Wethered and run by Levi White who

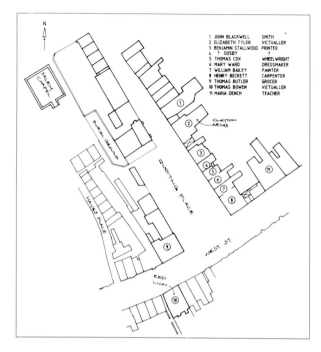

N

1 JOHN BLACKWELL	SMITH
2 ELIZABETH TYLER	VICTUALLER
3 BENJAMIN STALLWOOD	PRINTER
4 ? GOSBY	?
5 THOMAS COX	WHEELWRIGHT
6 MARY WARD	DRESSMAKER
7 WILLIAM BAILEY	PAINTER
8 HENRY BECKETT	CARPENTER
9 THOMAS BUTLER	GROCER
10 THOMAS BOWEN	VICTUALLER
11 MARIA DENCH	TEACHER

came from Little Marlow. White was married and it seems that the ale-house acted as a lodging house since the census records list four men who completed the household: a shoemaker, a carpenter, a farm labourer and a postman. Among the men who sold beer were James Allum, who was also a grocer, and John Stephenson, the same man who is mentioned in Directories as running the Coach and Horses.

There were several schools in West Street. More information about some of them is given in the section on schools but it is worth mentioning that there were day schools for small numbers of children, almost certainly held in private houses, of which very few details are known. The Directory for 1851 lists Caroline Anthony as running a day school; she was the stationer already mentioned. John Sharp, also listed as providing a day school, gives his occupation as schoolteacher in the census return. The Washbourne sisters lived on the north side of West Street, close to the Market Square. Ann had been born in London and was thirty-nine, while her sister

Elizabeth had been born in Marlow eleven years later. In 1842 Ann was a satin-stitch worker and also ran a children's bed-linen warehouse. She called herself an embroideress in 1851, but Elizabeth was described as a governess and they had an assistant living in their house as well as a servant. Elizabeth's name appears in the Directory as running a day school. By 1853 both sisters' names appear. Elizabeth was still in Marlow over twenty years later, running a 'ladies' day school' and a Christian Knowledge Society depot.

The corner of Hayes Place in 1991. Drawn by Margaret Richardson

Buildings on the south side of West Street in 1991. The big double-fronted house is a solicitor's office, the next one a private house and the one on the right is The Centurion restaurant. In 1851 this was the Post Office. Drawn by Margaret Richardson

The north side of West Sreet
in 1943. The gables are
easily identifiable in 1991.
Reproduced by courtesy of
the Royal Commission on
the Historical Monuments of
England

Sources

Census Enumerators' returns for Great Marlow for 1851. Public Record Office London. HO 107 1719.
Great Marlow Church Rate Books. These are the rate books of a parish rate levied to pay off the loan twards the rebuilding of the church. They run from 1838 to 1870 and are now in the County Record Office. PR 140/4/1-33.
Langley, T., *The History and Antiquities of the Hundred of Desborough*, 1797.
Musson & Craven *Directory for Buckinghamshire* for 1853.
Pigot & Co.'s *Directories of Great Marlow* for 1823/4, 1830 and 1842.
Post Office Directory for Great Marlow, Bucks. for 1864.
Registers of All Saints Parish Church, Marlow.
Sheahan, J.J., *The History and Topography of Buckinghamshire*, 1862.
Slater's (late Pigot) *Royal National Commercial Directory and Topography*, 1851.
Victoria History of the County of Berkshire Vol. I, 1906.
Victoria History of the County of Buckingham Vol. III, 1925.

The River

Navigation

Much of Marlow's character arises from its situation on the Thames. Until the early nineteenth century the river was an important transport route for agricultural products, raw materials and coal carried up or down stream on barges capable of carrying from 50 to 200 tons of material. Navigation was not helped by the numerous mills and weirs along the river's course; grinding corn, making paper and catching eels and other fish were all useful activities, but the millers who controlled the weirs and sluices managed the water levels and flow rates in accordance with their own needs for water power rather than with any idea of meeting navigation requirements or minimising flooding. This conflict between local milling interests and the needs of navigation was never fully resolved and river transport rapidly lost out when the first railways began to appear in the 1830s.

General view of the river in 1850. Rock & Co London No 1505

The old weirs on the Thames incorporated flash-locks; these were through-ways made up of a series of vertical, removeable paddles which could be temporarily raised or removed to allow a barge to pass through. The difference in water levels on either side could be as much as two to three feet so the 'flash' of water when the paddles were raised was sometimes more like a surging torrent. Downstream traffic had to ride these flashes, while barges travelling upstream had to be pulled through, either by men with ropes or by one or more winches.

The water levels along the river were very variable, especially in the dry summers, and although the barges were limited to a draught of three to four feet, some river journeys took much longer than usual because of the need to lie up until the water was deep enough to allow for passage. The journey from Oxford to London usually took three to four days with the upstream journey taking five days. Up to the 1770s barges had usually been hauled by gangs of men, but with the introduction of proper towpaths it became feasible to use horses. When the towpath up to Marlow lock was installed, sometime after 1773, some rioting occurred as the towing gangs were displaced. Eventually the men received some form of compensation from the parish and from the Thames Commissioners.

Goods carried downstream from Marlow included corn, flour, malt and timber, while coal and rags for the paper mills came up from London. It may seem strange that coal had to travel upstream when so much came down the Oxford Canal from the Midlands, but apparently coal was not allowed to be carried further south than Reading. Passing traffic included stone for building and agricultural products such as cheese, wool and hay for London.

The overall tonnage carried on the Thames network in the early part of the nineteenth century is estimated to have been about 84,000 tons a year, representing about 800 barge journeys. This tonnage started to fall off by the 1840s as the railways competed for both passenger and goods traffic. The first Great Western Railway Bill in 1834 caused the Thames Commissioners considerable concern and they set aside £1,500 from their annual income of about £13,000 to oppose the Bill. But the railway was built, reaching Maidenhead in 1838, Twyford in 1839 and Bristol in 1840. A passenger service from Maidenhead to High Wycombe opened in 1854 with extensions to Aylesbury in 1862 and Oxford in 1864. The Maidenhead-High Wycombe line was rebuilt for goods operation in 1870 and the Bourne End to Marlow spur was added in 1873.

The Thames Commissioners responded to the threat posed by the railways by lowering tolls, but this reduced the money available for necessary repairs. By the 1850s the financial situation was serious and creditors' interest was reduced from 5% to 4% in 1853 and to a mere 1% by 1857. This was the year in which the Thames Conservancy was created. Initially it took over responsibility for the Thames below Staines, but by 1866 the Conservancy had the whole of the river in its care. By this time annual receipts had dwindled from £13,000 to £3,000 and considerable debts had accrued.

Marlow Bridge and Lock

The present bridge across the Thames was completed in 1831. Previous bridges were wooden, repairs being provided for in medieval times by rents from certain properties in Marlow, administered by bridge wardens. The site of these earlier bridges was downstream, in line with what is now St Peter's Street, formerly known as Duck Lane because of the public

Wooden bridge, probably the one demolished in 1789, running from the Berkshire side on the left over to Duck Lane. Note the eel bucks and the flash-lock, open to allow the passage of a boat. Reproduced by Brian Drage from a photograph of the original by Robert Ticehurst in the archives of the Marlow Society

ducking-stool on the river bank. High Street at that time ended in a wharf on the riverside. By the end of the eighteenth century it became necessary to replace the existing wooden bridge because it was no longer possible to repair it. Buckinghamshire County was asked to contribute to the cost but the magistrates ruled that, because certain lands and properties provided money towards the cost of the upkeep, the bridge was not the responsibility of the county. So money was raised by public subscription and a new wooden bridge was built, still on the old site, in 1789. The bargemasters had asked that the central navigable archway should be raised to give their barges more headroom, and the Thames Commissioners contributed £50 towards the cost of raising the arch by eighteen inches.

This bridge only lasted for about forty years and then needed to be replaced, perhaps reflecting increased traffic or that, for the most part, it had been built from wood used in the previous bridge. A report on its condition, made in August 1828, records that it would be:

> Best and cheapest in the end to build a
> New Bridge resting on the Buckingham
> shore at the wharf adjoining the

The end of St Peter's Street, said to have been painted by Frederick Warner (1840-1875) and known as 'Marlow Ferry'. Reproduced by Brian Drage from a photograph of the painting by Robert Ticehurst in the archives of the Marlow Society

Churchyard and on the Berks shore at Mr Rolls Wharf. If the expense is not too great a stone Bridge of five elliptical arches would be the most eligible, for there would not only be a grand entrance thrown open to the Town on the Buckshire side, but a great improvement in the Road on the Berks side.

The Buckinghamshire magistrates, who were the chief promoters of the scheme for this bridge, were impressed with the 'Grand Entrance' idea which reflected the national trend for improvement current at the time, even though this meant moving the site of the bridge; in any case the new line had the advantage that the old bridge could be used until the new one was ready. An Act of Parliament 'to defray the expences of Rebuilding Marlow Bridge' was passed in 1829 and an engineer, Millington, was appointed. He then gained another job and left, either before building work had begun or soon afterwards and William Tierney Clark was appointed as his successor. The Act apportioned financial liability to the two counties, one-fifth to Berkshire and four-fifths to Buckinghamshire, and also abolished the office of bridge warden. The last wardens were Sir William Clayton, Thomas Wethered and Thomas Rolls and the properties and lands which had provided some of the income were sold by auction in September 1829. Clark had just built a

Marlow suspension bridge, completed in 1831. This engraving by Tombleson was done before the new church was built, so must date from c.1833

suspension bridge at Hammersmith and his designs for the new Marlow bridge were exhibited at the Royal Academy in 1830. Later he was to build the bridge over the Danube linking Buda with Pest. Clark's contractors were Corby, who tendered for the brick-work, Clifford, who did the stone-work, and William Bond, for timber-work, all Marlow men. The iron-work was carried out by William Hazeltine of Shrewsbury.

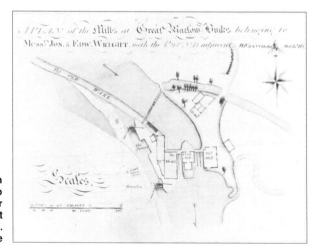

Plan of Marlow mills, drawn in 1816 by W. Francis who was at the time Master of Sir William Borlase School. It shows the first pound lock. Photograph by Brian Drage

The first pound lock was opened in 1773 to the south of the weir. Pound locks are familiar sights on rivers and canals today and consist of an area of water which is confined by two sets of moveable gates. At one end the water level within the lock is the same as that in the main stream and these gates are opened first to allow a barge or boat to enter the lock. The gates at that end are then closed and the gates at the other end are opened, allowing the water level inside the lock to rise or fall in order to reach the same level as the main stream again. The barge can then continue on its journey. Marlow's first lock was turf-sided and required quite a lot of maintenance. Rollers were provided at certain key positions to help to guide the upstream traffic into the lock. From there on barges had to be hauled up to what was called Rose's Wharf by a complicated system of winches. It is possible that the wharf was actually Rolls' wharf, and belonged to the brothers John and Thomas Rolls, who were coal merchants. Very long lines, of up to five hundred yards in length, had to be used because of the lack of any towing path between the lock and the wharf. The toll was initially one penny but was raised to fourpence in 1779. The second lock, on the present site, was built in 1825. It was made of Headington stone and cost £4,686.

The second pound lock, probably c.1920. Reproduced by courtesy of Buckinghamshire County Museum

Marlow Mills

Early in the eighteenth century the three mills at Marlow were described as a thimble mill, a corn mill and an oil mill. Thimbles were manufactured by John Lofting and the oil mill was used for the extraction of oil from rape seed. The corn mill was probably the most important and continued in use until the beginning of this century. The weir at that time ran right down to the thimble mill and the only route up or down stream was through the flash-lock in the centre. Barges travelled downstream with the flow of water when the tackle was raised and were winched upstream with the aid of the capstan situated near the bottom of St Peter's Street. The bridge over the river was much nearer the weir at that time and the negotiation of both the low bridge arch and the flash-lock was tricky and on occasions disastrous.

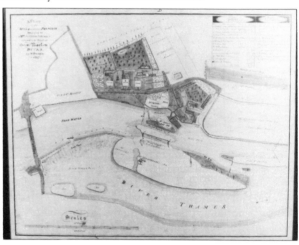

Early plan of the mills at Great Marlow, drawn by W. Francis in 1827. Photograph by Brian Drage

The force of the water which fed the mill-race was sufficient to drive several wheels and both the oil mill and the thimble mill were converted into paper mills. That this had been achieved by the end of the eighteenth century is clear from a Sun Fire Insurance Policy of 2 April 1776, in the name of Thomas Rickett of Great Marlow, paper maker and mealman, which insures

> *his Dwelling house, paper finishing*
> *Room and Drying loft*   *£350*

Water Paper Mill separate   £300
new Water Paper Mill separate from the
above adjoining the Pound Lock   £350
Water Corn Mill separate   £250
Utensils and stock, going gears included   £50
All brick timber and tiled

Mr Rickett must have died in 1797 because a notice in the *Reading Mercury* of 8 January 1798 advertises an auction sale at Garraways Coffee House, Change Alley, London on 9 February of the same year 'by order of the Executors of Mr Thomas Rickett, deceased'. The sale is of

> *The freehold estate comprising Two Paper Mills, a Corn Mill and premises in the occupation of Messrs. Wright, with the Bucks. Fishery and valuable Lock at Great Marlow in the Co. of Bucks. with two Wheel races, a powerful head of water, large Water Wheels and Tackle, Paper Engines, Vats, Chests and Presses*

The Wrights, Edward and Joseph, both master paper makers,had obviously been tenants of Mr Rickett and it seems that they then bought the mills, since a Royal Exchange Fire Insurance Policy of 7 October 1803 is in the names of 'Edward and Joseph Wright of Great Marlow, Paper Makers, as Proprietors, and George Dean of the parish of Hambledon, as Mortgagee, both of the County of Bucks.' The corn mill was leased to Greenaway Jaques, who was insuring the contents in 1803. He was succeeded by John Jaques by 1823 and then by William Jaques by 1830.

General view of Marlow Mills, exact date unknown, showing the end of Pepper's paper mill on the left and the corn mill. The other paper mill buildings are behind the tree on the right. Reproduced by courtesy of Buckinghamshire County Museum

77

The Wrights took an apprentice, Francis Pepper, in 1798; either this, or a later partnership, was dissolved 'by mutual consent' on 5 July 1814, according to the *London Gazette* of 25 October of that year. Francis Pepper then seems to have bought one of the paper mills, since in 1823 he is listed, together with Edward and Joseph Wright, as a paper maker at Marlow Mills.

In 1826 there was a disastrous fire which involved the mill belonging to the Wrights. It seems to have started at both ends of the building at the same time and to have caused a great deal of damage. The account says that

> by great exertions the paper mills of Mr
> Pepper and his residence, and the flour
> mill of Mr Jaques were preserved

and seems to suggest that the fire may have been started deliberately, perhaps as a protest against the use of machinery in the Wrights' mill. It is worth mentioning that Marlow was also involved to some extent in the Swing riots of 1830, when farmers and paper makers were the subject of letters threatening to destroy their crops and buildings if their machines were not removed; Richard Webb, a farmer of Marlow Bottom, received such a letter.Returning to the fire at the Wrights' mill, as much as 320 reams of paper were said to have been destroyed. The building had presumably to be repaired or rebuilt and it seems as if this was also the time when another paper mill building was erected by the Wrights to the east of the one which was damaged by the fire.

So the situation in 1830 was that paper making was carried on by the Wrights – by then Joseph and William – and Francis Pepper, with the corn mill being owned by the Wrights and leased to William Jaques. Pepper died in March 1831 and the *Reading Mercury* of 13 June of that year gives details of the sale of

> a capital mill at Great Marlow, on the
> banks of the Thames, Buckinghamshire,
> with immediate possession, comprising
> a Paper Mill with a powerful head of
> water, spacious engine, bleaching and
> rag houses, and other premises. Also a
> residence.

No immediate sale took place, since the same newspaper gave notice on 30 April the following year that the sale would be by auction at the Mart, London, on 18

Corn Mill, Great Marlow, 1938. Photograph by S.H. Freese; reproduced from the J.H. Venn, S.H. Freese collection

May 1832.

The Wrights then bought Pepper's mill and from 1838 onwards the records show that paper manufacture was carried on by the two of them. At the time of the census, in 1851, the firm was said to be employing twenty men and twenty-four women and boys. Joseph Wright, aged fifty-one, lived in his own house with his family. He had been married to a girl from Hackney in 1823, but the marriage was not a happy one. In 1833 a female servant, Rose Folly, entered the Wrights' service. Mrs Wright sacked her in 1835 and started divorce proceedings against her husband for cruelty and adultery. He refused her access to their children and his workpeople seem to have treated her in a very ignominious manner; his foreman, Joseph Eagle, is reported as having shaken a stick at Mrs Wright on one occasion in the presence of her husband. There is a Joseph Eagle included in the census returns; he was sixty-six in 1851 and was then a grocer in Spittal Street, so he had obviously changed his job. Two daughters and a son are recorded as living at The Mills with Joseph Wright, who is described as married, but no wife is included; the household was completed by a twenty-year-old female servant. William Wright, Joseph Wright's brother and partner, was fifty-three. William's wife, Mary, was fifteen years younger than her husband and they had five children, aged from eight to under a year. The household was completed by two servants, both girls of eighteen who had been born in Great Marlow.

William Jaques, whose occupation is given as corn miller employing three men, was still unmarried at thirty-seven and he also had a servant to look after him. Others living in the area of the mills at the time of the census were two men of independent means, Thomas Fenn and Ralph Rose, both listed as proprietors of houses and both born outside the county. Rose lived in a house which he himself owned but Fenn lived in a house owned by the Wrights. Benjamin Parslow, a timber merchant, also lived there with his family in a house owned by the Wrights. It seems from later records that there was a saw mill amongst the complex of buildings and perhaps Mr Parslow was running this. One of the Wrights' other employees is listed as living in Mill Yard, James Bird, a paper maker, his wife Emily who was a paper sorter and

The Sycamores, Mill Road, home of Mrs Josiah Wright around 1900. Drawn by Margaret Richardson

Corn and paper mills, Great Marlow, 1938. Photograph by S.H. Freese; reproduced from the J.H. Venn, S.H. Freese collection

Weir Cottage in 1991, said to have been built by the Wright family but lived in by Greenaway Jaques from 1803 according to the deeds. Drawn by Margaret Richardson

their six children. Mr Jaques's tenants included John Rockey, who lived at Mill Cottage with his wife and four children, and William Barton, listed as a manufacturer of sewed muslin. He and his wife had five daughters at home, ranging in age from eighteen to thirty-seven, of whom only the oldest was married. In spite of this, or perhaps because of it, Mr Barton's household included one servant. None of this family was born in the county, the three younger children having been born in Hackney.

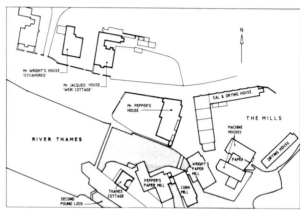

The lock-keeper was Joseph Coster, who was twenty-eight in 1851 and came from an old Marlow family. His wife had been born in Shoreditch but all four Coster children had been born in Marlow. The family lived in the lock-house. The lock-keeper's wages seem to have been £3 a month but Thacker records that Coster was deprived of this sum in 1854 'because of the competition of the railways'. He was, however, allowed to continue to live in the lock-house and to keep the pleasure tolls in return for seeing that the traffic passed safely through the lock and for generally looking after it.

Occupations

Occupations linked in some way with the river would seem to be paper making, receiving and distributing coal, boat and barge building, rope making and milling corn. The numbers of men following these occupations is very small, confirming the fall-off in importance of the river as a major transport route.

Four men gave their occupation as coal merchant and two of them, John and Thomas Rolls, had wharfage down on the river side. Twelve men said that they were coal porters and one was recorded as a coal packer. Presumably the coal was distributed from the wharf by horse and cart but no coal draymen appear in the census returns.

Rope making must have been dying out; only four men said that they were rope makers, though one said that he was a rope spinner and another that he was a rope maker's labourer.

The paper manufacturers were Joseph and William Wright and Thomas and William Weedon. The Weedons were at Temple and the Wrights at Marlow. Eighteen men said that they were paper makers and a further eight that they were paper mill labourers. There were two engineers at the mills and several women were recorded as rag sorters, rag pickers, paper sorters and paper pickers.

Boats and barges seem surprisingly little in evidence. One man is recorded as a boat builder and one as a barge builder, though eleven men call themselves bargemen and four are given as barge carters. There were two wharfingers, men who operated wharves on the river side. William Jaques features as a corn miller and maybe the 'mill wright' and 'mill labourer' helped to make up his labour force rather than that of the Wrights.

Many men in Marlow gave their occupation simply as labourer. This makes it impossible to tell in what role they were employed. A large number of them probably worked as agricultural labourers and others worked in the Wethered brewery. Others again may have turned their hands to whatever jobs were available and some of these may have been connected with the river. But the overall impression is that apart from work at the mills the Thames provided few job opportunities in the mid-nineteenth century.

Leisure

The Thames had been popular with anglers over the centuries as the following extract from the *Windsor and Eton Express* for 10 January 1852 shows:

THE PIKE.

> *SUCCESSFUL ANGLING A short time since the fisherman to Major General Sir R.W.Clayton, Bart., of Harleford, near this town, took a very fine jack which weighed 27 ½ pounds; it is a handsome fish; also a very large otter captured at the same place, have been preserved and stuffed in a manner creditable to Mr R.Harding, at whose house in High Street, they are now to be seen. The above is only one of the numerous fish taken in this neighbourhood – the river abounds in them. A few days since W.Hickman, Esq., of this town took three, weighing together 42 lbs.*

Other evidence for leisure activities related to Marlow itself seems to be non-existent for the mid-nineteenth century. The presence of boats is implied by the leisure tolls which Joseph Coster was allowed to keep when he was no longer paid a monthly salary but, unlike Henley, Marlow was not then developing into a fashionable riverside town. This was to happen later, in Edwardian times, when the fashion was to rent houses along the river bank and the change may have started with the establishment of Marlow's own Regatta. A meeting was held in the Town Hall on Monday 7th August 1865 to consider the desirability of having an annual Regatta and a provisional committee was set up 'to ascertain the feelings of the neighbourhood on this point, to collect subscriptions and to report to a public Meeting'. The committee members included three Wethereds, T.Rolls, T.Wright, R.Foottit, and G.S.Pearce and, as Secretary pro.tem., none other than William Lakin Ward.

Sir,

At a preliminary Meeting held at the Town Hall, Marlow, on Monday, the 7th instant, G. H. VANSITTART, Esq, in the chair, to take into consideration the feasibility of establishing a first class Regatta at Marlow, the following Resolutions were unanimously adopted :—

(1) " That it is desirable to establish an annual Regatta at Marlow, to commence in 1866, and that a Provisional Committee be formed to ascertain the feelings of the neighbourhood on this point, to collect subscriptions, and to report to a public Meeting :—

(2) " That the Provisional Committee consist of the following Gentlemen, Messrs. G. H. VANSITTART, J. CARSON, P. BORGNIS, T. O. WETHERED, O. P. WETHERED, J. S. CARSON, T. ROLLS, R. P. WETHERED, W. J. SHONE, T. WRIGHT, A. LAWRENCE, G. ROWLE R. FOOTTIT, G. S. PEARCE, J. ROBERTS, J. ADAMS, and R. H. SMITH.

In accordance with these resolutions the Provisional Committee met on the 16th instant, when it was resolved that a circular should be sent to the inhabitants of Marlow and its neighbourhood, soliciting Donations and Subscriptions for the several Cups and Prizes to be offered for competition and towards the annual expenses.

Will you have the kindness to inform me if you will afford the Regatta your pecuniary support —

It is proposed to offer Challenge Cups of the following values.

A CHALLENGE CUP value 100 Guineas.

" STEWARDS' " " 80 "

" LADIES' " " 60 "

" TOWN " " 50 "

also Presentation Cups and other Prizes.

I am Sir,

Your obedient servant,

W. L. WARD.

Secretary Pro. Tem.

O. B. Pearce, Printer, and Bookseller, Marlow.]

Copy of a letter seeking support for the establishment of Marlow's own Regatta. Reproduced by courtesy of Marlow Rowing Club

Sources

Bridgewardens' accounts, now in the County Record Office, B/142/1.
Defoe, D., *Tour through the Whole Island of Great Britain*, Everyman edition 1975.
Freese, S.J., typescript papers on the Marlow Mills; the originals are now in the Science Museum but there are copies in the County Record Office.
Karau, P., & Turner, C., *The Marlow Branch*, n.d. but c.1984.
Phillips, G., *Thames Crossings*, 1981.
Thacker, F.S., *Thames Highway*; two volumes published by the author 1914-1920.

Inns, Ale-houses and Beer sellers

As much of the history of England has been brought about in public houses as in the House of Commons. (Sir William Harcourt 1872)

Public houses play a larger part in the lives of the people than clubs or friendly societies, churches or missions, or perhaps than all put together. (Charles Booth 1889)

Like many nineteenth-century towns, Great Marlow was well-provided with inns and ale-houses. They served as meeting-places, starting-places for coaches and carriers, auction-rooms and venues for old-style games and other communal recreational activities as well as providing drink.

Inns were large, fashionable establishments with residential accommodation and, in the case of inns on main highways, often substantial coaching accommodation also. They offered wine, ale and beer, together with quite elaborate food for prosperous travellers. In the eighteenth century there were also taverns selling wine to the wealthy but not offering the extensive accommodation of inns. By the early part of the nineteenth century the tavern as a distinct institution had largely disappeared and most of the houses so-called were almost indistinguishable from the larger ale-houses. These ale-houses served ale or beer and provided basic food for the less well-off customers and were far more numerous than the inns.

Full publican's licences were granted at the General Annual Licensing Meeting, better known as Brewster Sessions, by licensing justices subject to conditions set out in the Alehouse Act of 1828. It is interesting that the word 'brewster' means 'a woman that brews ', indicating the significant part played by women in the home-brewing of ale. A major change came about in 1830. The Duke of Wellington's Beerhouse Act of that year allowed householders who were assessed for the poor rate to sell beer on payment of two guineas. This Act may have been in part a response to the pressure on the government to repeal the tax on beer, but was also an attempt to discourage the sale of spirits. Beer-houses catered for the poorer members of society, a reflection both of their prices and the very basic services which they offered. Since there was no need to obtain a licence from the justices, merely the need to pay the two guineas, the number of beer-houses was considerable. The houses were not allowed to open before 4 am and had to close at 10 pm. They were also to remain closed, as were ale-houses, during Divine Service on Sundays, on Christmas Day and on Good Friday.

Street frontage of Wethered's brewery, 1991. Drawn by Margaret Richardson

The main supplier of beer in Marlow was, of course, Thomas Wethered and Sons. Thomas had died in 1849 and in 1851 the brewery was being run by two of his sons, Owen, his eldest son, and Lawrence. The other brewer in the town was Richard Gibbons, aged sixty, who, as we have seen, lived in St Peter's Street with his wife Ann and their three sons and two daughters, all of whom were unmarried. Two of the sons, Edward and Charles, were brewer's assistants and the other son, Alfred, was a wine merchant's assistant. In the 1851 Directory John Gibbons is shown as a spirit merchant, living in West Street. He was sixty-six, so he could have been Richard's brother, employing his nephew, Alfred, as his assistant.

The breweries were a major source of employment

for people living in the town. In addition to the Wethered family and the Gibbons family there were five brewer's clerks, three brewer's draymen, twenty-five brewer's labourers and three coopers. Interestingly, all these people lived in the central part of the town, covered by Groups 1 and 2 of the census. Most of them were living in houses owned by Wethered, Williams or Clayton but even so it is evident that work in the brewery often carried with it an address in one of the main streets.

Entries in the Rate Book show the differences in scale of operation of the two Marlow brewers. The description of the Wethered brewery occupied two and a half pages:

Stoneware jar from
Wethered's brewery.
Photograph by Brian Drage

Name of occupier	Name of owner	Description of Property rated	Situation of Property	Rateable value
Wethered, Owen	Wethered	House, garden and orchard	High Street	£59.10
		Additional buildings	High Street	£ 1.14
Wethered, Owen & Lawrence	Wethered	3 rooms large	High Street	£29.15
		Building and Counting House Coopery, scalding Sheds, Drayhouse and Stables	High Street	£ 6.16
		2 Stables and Cart House	High Street	£ 6.16
		Malthouse, Store Ho. & Carpenter's Shop	High Street	£15.16
		Table beer Tun Room with loft over	High Street	£10.04
		Brewhouse buildings with malt lofts & Engine House	High Street	£85.00
		Timber yard, saw pit, Piggery & Store Room for timber	High Street	£ 8.10
Wethered, Owen & Lawrence	Davenport	Store room	Pound Lane	£ 2.2.6
	TPWilliams	Malthouse and sheds	Lowes Yard	£12.15
		Store House three Stables and Loft	Maddocks Yard	£17.00
	Wethered	Cellar	West Street	£ 2.11
		Malthouse	Camden's Yard	£12.15
		Storehouse & Lofts	Adjoining Withers	£ 2.11
	TPWilliams	2 Storehouses Loft & Small Garden	In garden	£ 2.11
		2 Large Stables, Loft	Burrells Yard	£ 3.08
		2 Stables Coachhouse Dungyard, Piggery Cart Shed & Storeroom	Burrells Yard	£10.04
		Small Storehouse	In yard	£ .17
	Wethered	Malthouse, Barley Lofts & Coal House	Bottom of High Street	£21.05
		Screening Rooms, Lofts & Malt Rooms	Bottom of High Street	£17.00

Note:The entries go on to include land, sometimes described as meadow or orchard.

Name of occupier	Name of owner	Description of Property rated	Situation of Property	Rateable value
Gibbons, Richard	Gibbons	House Garden Malt house Brewery, yard, Stables & Store Rooms	St Peter St	£34.17
		Store Rooms	St Peter St	£ 7.4.6
	Exs of the late S Baines	Malthouse	St Peter St	£12.15

88

In 1851 Marlow had two inns in the town, The Crown and The Greyhound. A third inn, The Complete Angler on the Berkshire bank in Bisham, can also be thought of as a 'Marlow' inn and indeed is often so described and listed.

The Crown in Market Place is listed in Slater's 1851 Directory as a family and commercial hotel, posting-house and Inland Revenue Office. It was run by Thomas Furnell, unmarried and aged 34. He had been born in Great Marlow. On the day of the census only one visitor was listed, a commercial traveller in drapery called Nicholas Reed. Staff at the Crown included housekeeper, horse keeper, cook, chambermaid, housemaid and flyman. The Crown served as an important meeting-place and focus for many activities in the town, including political meetings and petty sessions. A coach, The Wonder, left the Crown Hotel each weekday morning at a quarter past eight for Maidenhead to connect with trains on the Great Western Railway.

The Crown Hotel and Market Place in 1859. Rock & Co London No. 4092

The Greyhound in Spittal Street was a coaching inn with a narrow passage by the side to allow the coaches to reach the yard at the back. It was run by George Abbott, aged 40, who had been born in Streatley, and his wife Mary, aged 35, from Basingstoke. The Abbotts had three young children, Ann 8, Jane 6 and George aged 2. The census also records a male house servant and a waggoner.

The Greyhound was the starting-place for several carrier routes. Omnibuses ran each weekday morning to Maidenhead and Windsor 'at a quarter before seven' to connect with trains. Farley's Van, which also stopped at the Three Tuns in West Street, ran to Henley on Tuesday and Thursday evenings and to Wycombe 'every Tuesday and Friday forenoon about eleven'. Richard Robinson, a carrier, also operated from The Greyhound to London, Maidenhead, Salt Hill, Slough and Colnbrook every Monday and Thursday.

The Complete Angler, the third of Great Marlow's inns, was on the Berkshire side of the river. It was run by Hezekiah Parslow who appears in Slater's 1851 Directory as a timber merchant living in West Street; he is similarly listed in Pigot's Directory for 1842. He is not recorded in the Great Marlow census returns, but is in the returns for Bisham – in fact he was the enumerator for his area. He was thirty-six and is described as an innkeeper. His wife Mary Ann, who was ten years older than her husband, was born in Great Marlow and seems to have been married before. Two of her children from her first marriage and a six-month old daughter of her second make up the family. There were three servants, two visitors and a lodger – a carpenter whose name was Creswell, perhaps a relative of the previous landlord, William Creswell, who was running the inn in 1842. By 1851 William, aged 71 and widowed, was living in High Street being looked after by Sarah Butler, his housekeeper. The Creswell family was a large one, including John Creswell, baker, James Creswell, carpenter, and George and William Creswell, coal merchants with wharfage on Thames side. George Creswell also ran The Swan. There is a Parslow family listed in the Marlow census, living in the Mills, of whom Benjamin Parslow gives his occupation as timber merchant and it is seems likely that he was a relative of Hezekiah.

It was quite common for people who ran ale-houses or sold beer to have another occupation as well. Apart from George Creswell, Henry Meakes who ran the Cross Keys in Spittal Street was a smith; Henry Neighbour of the Waterman in St Peter's Street was a cordwainer; William

The Complete Angler in 1859, after an illustration in *The Book of the Thames* by Mr & Mrs S.C. Hall. Drawn by Margaret Richardson

The Red Lion in West Street.
Reproduced by Brian Drage
from a photograph by Robert
Ticehurst in the archives of
the Marlow Society

Plumridge of the White Hart in Chapel Street was a bricklayer and Thomas Bowen, who ran the Red Lion in West Street, was the town's Surveyor. George Wyatt, who ran the Horns tavern in Chapel Street, also operated a carrier service, the Wagon, on Monday and Friday to London, Maidenhead, Salt Hill, Slough and Colnbrook. Mr Wyatt was a widower of 53 who lived with his unmarried son, James, and his daughter Rose, aged seventeen. Charles Wyatt, of West Street, gives his occupation as carrier, and was probably helping with the Wagon, since he is listed with Richard Robinson as the two carriers in the 1853 Directory. Again the Wyatt name features several times in the census returns.

The Red Lion in 1991. Drawn
by Margaret Richardson

Women played a significant role in the operation of drinking-houses. They helped their husbands, as did other members of the family, and this was probably particularly necessary for those men with other occupations. In 1851 two women are recorded as running public houses. Martha Ruddle was at the Hare and Hounds at Redpits, although the census returns give

91

MARLOW and MAIDENHEAD COACHES.

WYATT AND CLARK,

Respectfully announce to the Inhabitants and Families of MARLOW, MAIDENHEAD, and their Vicinities, that

FOR THE WINTER SEASON,

Their LIGHT POST COACH will leave the Crown Inn, MARLOW, at half-past Ten, every Monday, Wednesday, and Friday ; and return from the New Inn, Old Bailey on the alternate days, at a quarter past Ten, and the White Horse Cellar, Piccadilly, at Eleven precisely.

The ORIGINAL COACH will leave MARLOW on Monday Mornings at Five o'Clock, and return from the New Inn, Old Bailey, at half-past Two, and the White Horse Cellar, at a quarter past Three ; and, for the Winter Season, the Seven o'Clock Coach will be discontinued on Monday, but will run the other days, as usual, at Seven o'Clock, Sundays excepted.

Part of a bill advertising the service run by Wyatt & Clark. Reproduced by Brian Drage from a photograph of the original by Robert Ticehurst in the archives of the Marlow Society

Elizabeth Ruddle, aged 19, as the head of the household, with two sisters – Emma 17 and Eliza aged 13. Elizabeth gives her occupation as victualler, so perhaps her mother was away. Elizabeth Hobbs took over the running of the Two Brewers in St Peter's Street after her husband died and it is clear from a comparison between the census returns and the 1853 Directory that other women had done the same. Elizabeth Tyler took over the Clayton Arms in Quoiting Place, Mary Meakes succeeded to the Cross Keys in Spittal Street and Jane Reeves was running the Ship in West Street.

It is not always easy to pick up information about beer sellers and beer-houses from the census returns. Additional detail can be collected from a study of the various directories. Once the names of beer sellers are known it is then possible to do a cross check with the census returns and this often reveals that, not surprisingly, most of them had only recorded their other occupations. It seems that the number of beer sellers remained consistently around thirty in Great Marlow from the time of the 1830 Act until the beginning of the 1890s. After that they gradually decreased until only six were listed in Kelly's Directory for 1935, although some of the earlier beer-houses had developed into public houses. In general beer-houses were located in the poorer parts of the town, serving the working class areas. As can be seen from the following table there were seven in Dean Street and only one in High Street. There were several lodging-houses in

Dean Street and some of the lodging-house keepers were
also beer sellers.

Name	Occupation	Location
Beaver, William	Paper mill labourer	Chapel Street
Beckett, Henry	Carpenter/beer seller	Quoiting Place
Beckett, Samuel	Journeyman carpenter, beer seller	Dean Street
Boulter, John	Beer seller	Oxford Road
Carr, George	Lodging-house keeper	Dean Street
Clark, George	Journeyman carpenter	Dean Street
Cooper, James	Journeyman carpenter	Spittal Street
Croxon, William	Bargeman/beer seller	Dean Street
Davis, William	Agricultural labourer	Bovingdon Green
Earis, Joseph		Handy Cross
East, Joseph	Gardener	Dean Street
Green, Richard		West Street
Haines, Charles	Shoemaker	Chapel Street
Harding, William	Shoemaker	High Street
Humphreys, Jeremiah	Lodging-house keeper	Dean Street
Johnson, George	Gardener	West Street
Johnson, James		Chapel Street
Miatt, Joseph		Flackwell Heath
Oxlade, Richard		St Peter Street
Piggott, Robert	Brewer's labourer	West Street
Price, William	Lodging-house keeper	Dean Street
Rockell, Robert	Retailer of beer	Spittal Street
Smith, Diana		Chapel Street
Sparks, William	Victualler	Church Passage
Stephenson, Alice		West Street
Stroud, Henry	Bricklayer	Common Slough
Ward, Elizabeth	House servant	Quoiting Place
Way, Robert	Brewer's labourer	Strong Beer Acre
White, John	Bargeman	St Peter's Street

Notes: The list of names is taken from Slater's Directory for 1851, under the
heading Retailers of Beer. The occupation is as given in the census return.

Many of the early beer-houses took on names,
including Alma, Bank of England, Bricklayer's Arms,
Crown and Anchor, Crown and Cushion, Fox and
Pheasant, Jolly Cricketers, Queen, Travellers' Rest and so
on. Some of these remain today as public houses while
others have disappeared.

Beer-houses were sometimes the scene of misdemeanours and family rows. Two extracts from the *Bucks Advertiser and Aylesbury News* will illustrate this. A report for 21 June 1851 reads:

> *Charles Haines, of the Bear, Marlow, was charged with allowing card playing in his house, contrary to the tenor of his licence. Fined 40s. and costs.*
> *Robert Piggott, of the Blue Bonnet, Marlow, with a like offence. Fined 40s. and costs.*
> *Henry Neighbour, landlord of the Waterman, Marlow, charged with a like offence. Fined 40s. and costs.*
> *It was remarked by the bystanders as being singular that all the parties summoned happened to be of the opposite party to the constables, and in dealing with the blue or liberal brewer of course the constables were doing their duties fairly and impartially.*

There is an interesting play on words here, since the two parties in Marlow were known as 'Coppers' or Tories, supporters of Williams, and 'Blues' or Reformers, who supported Clayton. Robert Piggott lived in a house which was owned by Clayton and both Charles Haines and Henry Neighbour lived in houses owned by Richard Gibbons, Marlow's other brewer, who was presumably also a Clayton supporter.

The other account appears in the edition on 15 November 1851:

> *Eliza Coleshill charged William Bowles, her brother, with assaulting her. She went to the house of her brother with her husband and called for a pint of beer; when the beer was brought into the tap-room, the husband said 'put it up'; Bowles refused, the score being already too long. A regular scuffle and angry words ensued. Bowles alleged that he did no more than was necesary to get them out of the house. He said that his witness had given him the slip after calling to lunch with him, so that he had no one to contradict his sister, who swore that he assaulted her. Fined 1s.*

Inn signs, 1991. Photographs by Peter Diplock

94

and costs.

Eliza Coleshill lived in Gun Lane with her husband; she was a lace maker and he was a fruiterer. There are several men called William Bowles so it is not easy to say which one was Eliza's brother. None of them specifically say that they are beer sellers, but the mention in the newspaper account of the tap-room suggests that William Bowles ran some sort of beer-house. The most likely men are William Bowles of Gun Lane who was an agricultural labourer or William Bowles of Common Slough who was a shoemaker.

Many of the ale-houses and beer-houses which feature in the census returns for 1851 are still in Marlow today; they include The Chequers, The Ship, The Red Lion and the Two Brewers. Others have disappeared, e.g. The Greyhound and The Waterman's Arms. The latter was purchased by Thomas Somers Cocks and was adapted to form bachelors' quarters as an overflow from the main house, then Thames Bank and now Thames Lawn, and coachman's quarters.

There seems to be no evidence in the mid-nineteenth century for any strong temperance movement. Possibly this is because any such development came later or perhaps such records as may have existed have not been found.

Tamsin House in Chapel Street, 1991. Over the ground-floor window and below the sign is a painted inscription, showing that at one time beer was sold. The house may have been The Black Horse. Photograph by Bill Purser

Detail of the inscription which reads: LICENSED TO SELL BEER BY RETAIL AND TO DEAL IN TOBACCO. Photograph by Bill Purser

Door of private house in Station Road, which was at one time the Wheatsheaf. Photograph by Peter Diplock, 1991

Sources

Clark, P., *The English Alehouse – a social history 1200-1830*, 1983.
Cocks, A.H., 'A note concerning two Marlow prints', *Records of Buckinghamshire* vol.X, no.6 (1915), 380-389.
Dixon, P., 'Brewers, Pubs and Temperance Societies in High Wycombe 1812-1929'. Dissertation submitted for the Certificate in Local History, Oxford University Department for External Studies, 1985.
Monckton, H.A., *A History of English Ale and Beer*, 1966.
Monckton, H.A., *A History of the English Public House*, 1969.

Politics

Great Marlow was represented in Parliament from 1299, but ceased sending members in 1308. From this date until 1623 there are no records of representatives of the borough, but in the Parliament held in the twenty-first year of the reign of James I (1622-23) the case for getting the right of representation restored was taken up by Mr Hakevill of Lincoln's Inn. He discovered that three boroughs in Buckinghamshire – Amersham, Great Marlow and Wendover – had had rights of representation at one time but had allowed them to lapse. Petitions were presented to the Commons then sitting to have the franchise restored. The King, apparently, was not pleased with the idea of even more burgesses, declaring that he was 'troubled with too great a number already'. But Mr Hakevill must have argued the case well for in 1623 Marlow was again entitled to send its two representatives to Westminster, Henry Borlase and Thomas Cotton in that year. The borough continued to exercise this right until 1867 when the number of its representatives was reduced to one, as a consequence of the Reform Act of that year. It finally lost its right to a Member of Parliament in 1885 when its representation was subsumed in that of the county.

The period which we have been studying is basically that between the two Reform Acts of 1832 and 1867, a period during which the public in general became more politically aware although there would still have been a large percentage of the population without the right to vote. Before 1832 Marlow was classed as a 'scot and lot' borough meaning that all men who paid the church rate were entitled to vote. In the case of Marlow this meant about 250 people but it would probably be a mistake to assume that the rest of the population were not interested in campaigning.

For most of the eighteenth century the Clayton family came nearest to providing Marlow with a patron. They owned a large number of houses in the borough and one of Marlow's two seats in Parliament was held by

Portrait of Thomas Williams of Llanidan by Sir Thomas Lawrence, thought to have been painted in 1787. Reproduced by permission of The National Museum of Wales

William Clayton from 1761 to 1783 and by his son from 1783 until 1790. In 1788 Thomas Williams, of Llanidan, Anglesey, bought the Temple Mills near Marlow. When Defoe visited the area in the 1720s the mills were renowned 'for making Bisham Abbey Battery work, viz. Brass Kettles and Pans etc. of all sorts'. Williams continued to manufacture brass and copper goods and was known as the copper baron of his day.

Thomas Williams became one of Marlow's MPs in 1790. He also started to acquire property in the town. By the 1820s it was reckoned that the Williams family owned about half of the houses in Marlow, which meant that they had a large number of tenants. These tenants were apparently given advantageous rates if they voted for their landlord's candidate, who was in many cases actually their landlord, and were said to be evicted if they did not.

The Williams family continued to dominate local politics in Marlow until the 1820s. Around the turn of the century Thomas Williams decided that he would rebuild the market-house which stood at the top of the High Street. He obviously realised that such a gesture could not fail to bring him and his family to the notice of all the people of the town. It seems likely that Samuel Wyatt, who built Temple House for Williams as his residence, was also the architect for the new market-house. Thomas Williams died before it was finished but his son, Owen Williams, who succeeded him in business and as one of the town's MPs, saw to it that the building was completed in 1807.

In 1820 the town was represented by Owen Williams, as usual, and also by his son, Thomas Peers Williams. Both were Tories, right wing Conservatives, while the Clayton family were Whigs or Liberals. At about this time there was a determined effort to break the hold of the Williams family on the borough. In the election of 1826 the candidates were Owen Williams, Thomas Peers Williams and an opposing Whig candidate, James Morrison. He received quite a lot of support from several leading local tradesmen in Marlow and from Dissenters. He was defeated but he did poll 99 votes to TP Williams's 128. So again there were two Williams MPs. They took their revenge on those of their tenants who had voted for Morrison and evicted many of them. Morrison, supported by Sir William Clayton, took up the cause of those who had been evicted. Although some Clayton property had been sold in the 1790s the family still owned a large number of houses in the town and in the area immediately round it and this property was put to good use.

Clayton stood as a candidate in 1830. Again the two Williams candidates got in, but Clayton received as many as 171 votes against the 192 which T.P. Williams polled. In 1831 feeling for reform was running high. The *Bucks Gazette* for Saturday 7 May reported on a reform meeting held in Marlow on the previous Thursday when Owen Williams 'refused to give the inhabitants the use of their own Town-hall on the occasion'. Clayton addressed the meeting 'on the subject of reform amidst three loud cheers, and pointed out the evils which had afflicted the country from the want of it'. The actual poll lasted for four days and at the end of it the results were

Owen Williams	*196*
Thomas Peers Williams	*192*
Sir William Clayton	*187*

Of Sir William's votes 170 were plumpers or voters who only voted for one candidate even though having the right to vote for two – what might be termed a protest vote. Because of the close result a scrutiny was called for and the *Bucks Gazette* for 21 May includes an article, dated 14 May, which gives the flavour of the time:

> *The scrutiny comes on next Tuesday, when we expect a curious expose of the borough machinery in this place. The examination of Mr Wethered, the great brewer here and the most active partizan of the Messrs. Williams, was a smart one, and some of the answers were perhaps not quite satisfactory. Probably the House of Commons may elicit something more. We anticipate a complete 'show-up', ere long, of the mal-practices, and 'NOTICE TO QUIT system', so notorious in this borough, which justice has not yet been able to expose as it deserves.*

The report of the scrutiny is factual and gives the final results as:

Owen Williams   *193*
Thomas Peers Williams   *189*
Colonel Clayton   *184*

An article in the same edition of the paper, which provides a racy commentary on this election, is worth quoting:

> *The election for Marlow has terminated, and two anti-reformers are again sent to parliament. Reform succeeded not here. The breath of freedom died upon the gale. Long and arduous was the struggle; great and glorious the exertion; but the oligarchical principle at last prevailed. We will now take a hasty review of some of the circumstances attending the election here. Let us in the first place see how those have acted who were loud and clamorous for REFORM! They said <u>we will never vote for Williams again – we will risk home, person and perish first.</u> What have they done? Belied themselves! Now for the out-voters – those who have no residence in the place, and whose names are an insult to the town and so many frauds upon the rate book! London, reforming London, has furnished a precious specimen in a person whose political principles have aways been most violent – a man who curses the aristocracy of the country – yes, Goswell Street has produced an acquaintance of Hardy and Horne Tooke, and Thelwall, who came down expressly to Marlow to give <u>two</u> votes against reform!! Chesham furnished another <u>free-man</u> for the same laudable purpose. Stevenage has the honour of finding a third. Colnbrook and Chesham by the most shameful connivance, produced a fourth; and to complete the <u>field</u>, the Temple manufactured a fifth. Thus was the majority of five eked out from the registration of ALIENS.*
>
> *On the scrutiny we will not say much, for we never again wish to witness such*

a loathsome scene of prevarication and
perjury. Knowing as we do the
machinery that 'works so well' for the
evil-doers, we must say a more shocking
exhibition of moral prostitution was
never displayed, than during the four
days scrutiny at Gt.Marlow, in 1831.

Owen Williams died quite soon after this election whereupon Sir William was allowed to take up the vacant seat without contest.

All these elections predated the Reform Act of 1832, one effect of which was to standardise the franchise for boroughs. It was to apply to all adult males who owned or occupied property worth at least £10 a year who had not been in receipt of poor relief in the previous twelve months. Any former electors who did not qualify under this new franchise were allowed to retain the right to vote for the rest of their lifetime. Marlow's electorate increased from the 250 or so scot and lot voters to about 450 under this enlarged franchise.

Another result of the Act was the need for lists of electors. Up to 1832 no official lists of voters existed. The numbers were small in most boroughs and those entitled to vote would have been well known. But larger numbers made lists necessary and the job of keeping these lists was usually given to the Overseers of the Poor who compiled the Rate Books. Voting was by signed ballot paper and the results were put up for all to see. This meant that friends and enemies, employers and employees, landlords and tenants could all see how individuals had voted.

Apart from electoral reform some of the other national issues in the 1830s and 1840s were the re-establishment by the Pope of Catholic bishoprics in England, often described in newspapers as papal aggression, and agricultural matters culminating in the repeal of the Corn Laws. An issue of particular interest in Great Marlow, with its large Dissenting population, was the abolition of church rates. The Dissenters had three main demands: an end to the Church of England's monopoly of the marriage service, a civil register of births, marriages and deaths, and the end of church rates. The first two demands were met in 1836 and the following year the government attempted to meet the third by proposing a measure to abolish church rates. Clayton, who was heavily rated as a large landowner, was in favour of abolition but the measure was defeated. As a result the *Aylesbury News* predicted that Clayton would soon be joined by another Liberal member to continue the fight for reform but this was not to be. He had come top of the poll in the 1835 election, with T.P. Williams holding the other seat. In 1841 the contest was close

Thomas Peers Williams	*Tory*	*233*
Sir William Clayton	*Whig*	*170*
Renn Hampden	*Tory*	*169*

In fact Clayton was unseated by a petition, initiated by Hampden because of the closeness of the vote. It was shown that Clayton's bailiff had bribed an insolvent butcher by supplying him with some of the Harleyford Southdown sheep, although the man had previously been refused credit. Since this accounted for the extra vote the seat went to Hampden. The evidence also showed that the Williams family let their houses at uneconomic rents and sometimes at totally fictitious ones, in order that their tenants should qualify as voters. It is also clear that the Wethered family, by far the largest employers in the town, backed the Williams faction. It was Wethered money which enabled the petition to be pressed to a satisfactory conclusion since they took over from Hampden when he could no longer afford to pay the costs. Incidentally this is the election referred to by the Clerk to the Board of Guardians, when he says in his report that all the parish registers and lists were retained in London for seven weeks or more.

In 1847 Williams, with the help of the Wethereds, introduced Lt.Col. Brownlow Knox, his cousin, as the second conservative candidate. Clayton stood again but he was beaten by Knox 179 to 161. Knox was the son of Owen Williams's sister and continued to represent Great Marlow until 1868 when he retired. He was in favour of national education on a religious basis and was instrumental in bringing Marlow up to the modern standards of nineteenth-century Britain. He supported the introduction of gas lighting and the coming of the railway.

Portrait of Jacob Bell in the Museum of the Royal Pharmaceutical Society of Great Britain. Reproduced by courtesy of the Society

In the election of 1852 Knox and T.P. Williams again won the seats, though there was a Whig candidate. This was Jacob Bell, who had been involved in a bribery case at St Albans. He had stood as a candidate there in 1850 and was actually elected. But it was shown that his agents had acted unscrupulously and the borough was disenfranchised. Bell was absolved of all blame and so stood at Marlow. The results in 1852 were

Thomas Peers Williams	*Tory*	*242*
Lt.Col. Brownlow Knox	*Tory*	*198*
Jacob Bell	*Whig*	*99*

Bell was much more of a nationally-known personality. He was the founder of the Pharmaceutical Society, a Fellow of the Chemical, Linnean and Zoological Societies and was a collector of works of art. He was

Electors' Christian & Surnames.	Addition, Profession, or Trade.	Place of Abode.	W	K	B
Gaskell, William Penn	Gentleman	Rolfe's hould			—
Gibbons, John	Grocer	West street			—
Gibbons, Richard	Brewer	St. Peter's street..			—
Gibbons, Thomas	Coal merchant	St. Peter's street..	—	—	
Gibbs, William	Clerk	High street	—	—	
Gosby, Thomas	Fruiterer	Quoiting place	—	—	
Gray, Benjamin Joseph	Tailor	High street	—		—
Gray, Thomas	Shoe maker	High street	—	—	
Green, John	Gentleman	Pinkney's Green, Bisham	—	—	
Green, Joseph	Wheelwright	Chapel street	—	—	
Greenslade, Thomas	Farmer	Homer's farm			—
Guy, John	Farmer	Aston Rowant, Oxon			—

Part of the poll showing how people voted. Photograph by Brian Drage

interested in the law of copyright as it affected artists and also spent considerable time endeavouring to amend the laws relating to the medical profession and pharmacy. His ventures into politics were all unsuccessful; after Marlow he failed to win the seat at Marylebone and died in 1859 when he was only 49.

We have been fortunate in having access to the voting records for Great Marlow for the elections of 1847 and 1852. By studying these it is possible to obtain a detailed picture of the composition of the voting electorate and of how individuals voted. When this information is set against occupation and property ownership some interesting trends emerge.

103

COPY OF THE POLL,

TAKEN AT THE ELECTION FOR TWO REPRESENTATIVES FOR THE

BOROUGH OF GREAT MARLOW,

ON FRIDAY, the 9th DAY of JULY, 1852.

CANDIDATES { THOMAS PEERS WILLIAMS, ESQUIRE.
LIEUT.-COL. BROWNLOW KNOX.
JACOB BELL, ESQUIRE.

Final State of the Poll — WILLIAMS 242
KNOX 198
BELL 99

NUMBER OF VOTERS ON REGISTER . . . . .
NUMBER OF VOTERS POLLED . . . . .

J. SMITH, PRINTER, STATIONER AND COPPER PLATE &c., MARLOW.

Copy of the poll taken at the election for two representatives for the Borough of Great Marlow in 1852. Photograph by Brian Drage

104

It seems that the number of men voting in Great Marlow in the elections who also feature in the Parish Rate Book, either as house owners or, more commonly, as tenants, is 236. In terms of occupational groups the voters divide up as shown in the following table:

Occupational Group	Number voting
1 Farmers and bailiffs	18
2 Agricultural workers	6
3 Traders	60
4 Craftsmen	85
5 Manufacturers	1
6 Industrial craftsmen	–
7 Professions	11
8 Clerical	8
9 Servants	12
10 Of independent means	9
11 Victuallers	16
12 Labourers	10

The main property owners in the town were T.P.Williams, himself one of the candidates, the Wethered family and Sir William Clayton, who, as we have seen, was unseated in the 1841 election but stood again in 1847. Property ownership is shown in the following table:

Ownership	Number of properties
T.P.Williams	92
Sir William Clayton	30
The Wethered family	18
Owner occupied	25
Miscellaneous	71

Since there was a Whig candidate in each of the two elections we have studied it is worth looking at the men who only voted for Clayton and Bell. They count as plumpers and the details are set out in the next table:

Name	Occupation	Property ownership	1847	1852
Agar, Francis	Farmer	Clayton	–	B
Beckett, Henry	Carpenter	Clayton	C	B
Blackwell, Richard	Bailiff	Henry Micklem	C	B
Bowles, James	Fruiterer	Self	C	B
Brangwine, George	Farmer	Self	C	B
Brown, James	Coal merchant	Clayton	C	B
Butler, Thomas	Grocer	Clayton	C	B
Carter, William	Servant	Clayton	C	B
Clayton, Sir William	Baronet	Self	C	–
Cockram, Joseph	Grocer	Clayton	C	B
Cooper, James	Carpenter	Charles Fletcher	C	B
Croxon, James	Baker	George Aveling	C	B
Gibbons, Richard	Brewer	Self	C	B
Greenslade, Thomas	Farmer	Mrs Rose	–	B
Harding, Benjamin	Shoemaker	Thomas Rolls	C	B
Herbett, Charles	Servant	Clayton	C	B
Horrod, Samuel	Gentleman	Mrs Bouverie	C	–
House, William	Gamekeeper	Clayton	C	B
Humphreys, William	Saddler	Rachel Hall	C	B
Johnson, James	Carrier	Richard Gibbons	C	B
Keene, Alfred	Farmer	Joseph White	–	B
Kidd, George	Grocer	Mrs Bennett	C	B
King, Richard	Farmer	Clayton	C	–
LLoyd, William	Butcher	Clayton	C	B
Meekes, James	Vet	Miss Ralfs	C	B
Morgan, John	Draper	Dean & Chapter, Bristol	C	B
Oxlade, Richard	Beer seller	Richard Lucas	C	B
Piggott, Robert	Brewer's lab.	Clayton	C	B
Plumridge, John	Bricklayer	Clayton	C	–
Plumridge, William	Bricklayer	Clayton(?)	C	–
Plumridge, William	Chairmaker	Michael Fryer	–	B
Price, William	Lodging house keeper	Clayton	C	B
Reading, John	Labourer	Clayton	C	B
Russell, Henry	Farmer	Clayton	C	B
Smith, Richard	Shoemaker	Self	C	B
Smith, Robert	Hairdresser	Dean & Chapter, Bristol	C	B
Spicer, Ralph	Solicitor	Clayton	C	B
Stallwood, Henry	Bailiff	William Bond	C	B
Stephenson, John	Publican	Clayton	C	B
Styles, Thomas	Minister	Wright's Executors	C	B
Truss, Jeffery	Shoemaker	Clayton	C	B
Tyler, William	Agent	Clayton	C	–
Wane, Isaac	Farmer	George Brangwine	C	B
Webb, Henry	Farmer	James Deane	C	–
Webb, James	Farmer	Ralph Harris	C	–

It is clear that the landlord/tenant relationship had some influence on the voting pattern; twenty-one of the forty-five men voting for Clayton/Bell lived in Clayton-owned property. Of the others, only four were owner-occupiers and the rest lived in property owned either by people sympathetic to the issues which Clayton supported or by people who did not live in Marlow itself and who were therefore less likely to influence the voting choices of their tenants.

Equally interesting are the split votes. The details are given on the next page. In this group Clayton owned eleven of the properties and T.P. Williams owned ten; it was probably in the interests of all these tenants to split their votes between the two parties. As for the others, so many of them were tradesmen or shopkeepers that they, too, probably needed to keep in with both sides. Ten men owned their own house and the other landlords included some who did not live in the town.

The degree to which employment exerted an influence of voting patterns is to some extent implicit but it is worth repeating that Wethereds were by far and away the biggest employers at the time. Williams had plenty of men working for him also but his main influence on the voting pattern in Marlow seems to have been related to his property ownership.

It is not possible to look at all the occupational groups in detail, but the farmers make an interesting set. Those who did not own their own farm had to be nominated by their landlords and had to have been in the occupancy of their land for at least two and a half years to qualify.

John Cheer, who voted for the Tory package, was a bailiff for the Wethereds at Town Farm. William Corby, farming his father's farm, voted as his father had done and as his brother did. William Crouch lived in a Williams' house and Thomas Oxlade must have been in sympathy with the Williams' views. Otherwise the farmers voted for Clayton in 1847 and often for Bell or Bell and Williams in 1852. Their reasons must have varied, but Brangwyn and Wane probably supported him because they were Dissenters. George and his wife were admitted to the United Reform Church in 1841 and Isaac Wane, who made the proposal for the reduction of the church rate from 3d.

Name	Occupation	Property ownership	1847	1852
Aldridge, Henry	Shoemaker	James Bird Brooks	C W	B W
Aldridge, James	Shoemaker	Elizabeth Carter	–	B W
Allum, James	Saddler	Francis Hone	–	B W
Allum, William	Tailor	Miss Ralfs	C W	–
Batting, Alfred	Ironmonger	T.P.Williams	C W	–
Beckett, James	Carpenter	Self	C W	B W
Bennell, Samuel	Wheelwright	Clayton	C W	B W
Blackwell, John	Smith	T.P.Williams	C W	B W
Brooks, James Bird	Baker	Self	C W	–
Brown, William	Shoemaker	John Griffiths	W K	B W
Creswell, James	Baker	T.P.Williams	C W	–
Creswell, James jnr	Butcher	T.P.Williams	C W	B W
Creswell, William	Shoemaker	Clayton	C W	B W
Croxon, William	Bargeman	Richard Lucas	C	K W
East, Joseph	Farmer	Dean & Chapter, Bristol	C W	K W
East, William	Butcher	T.P.Williams	C W	B W
Frost, Thomas	Farmer	Clayton	–	B W
Gibbons, John	Grocer	Self	C W	B
Gray, Joseph	Tailor	T.P.Williams	C	B W
Gray, Thomas	Shoemaker	Ralph Harris	C W	K W
Hackshaw, William	Sawyer	Great Marlow Parish	C	K W
Haines, Charles	Shoemaker	Richard Gibbons	–	B W
Harman, Robert	Corn Dealer	James Creswell	–	B W
Hickman, Thomas	Grocer	Self	C	B W
Hoare, Charles	Publican	T.P.Williams	C K	K W
Humphreys, Jeremiah	Lodging House Keeper	Self	C W	–
Hunt, James	Tailor	Mrs Lovegrove	C	B W
Jaques, William	Miller	Self	C W	B W
Johnson, William	Basket Maker	Thomas Corby	C	B W
Jones, David	Tailor	Clayton	C	B W
Keep, Henry	Hurdle Maker	Wethered	C W	B W
Lovegrove, Joseph	Grocer	Self	C W	B W
Mason, William	Draper	Alfred Batting	–	B W
Meadows, John	Gentleman	Hickman	C W	W
Meakes, Joseph	Smith	William Cox	C W	K W
Meekes, Joshua	Smith	T.P.Williams	C W	B W
Newell, Edward	Baker	Clayton	C	B W
Pepper, Joseph	Bricklayer	Benjamin Atkinson	C	B W
Piggott, Robert	Farm Labourer	Clayton	C	K W
Plucknutt, James	Baker	Rachel Hall	C W	B
Plumridge, Henry	Bricklayer	Benjamin Atkinson	–	B W
Pusey, William	Turner	William Cox	C W	B W
Reading, George	Bricklayer	Clayton	C	K W
Savage, William	Chairmaker	Clayton	C	B K
Sellman, William	Painter	C.H.Warcus	C	W
Simmonds, Joshua	Farmer	John Parker	C	K W
Stallwood, Benjamin	Printer	Clayton	C W	B W
Stroud, Henry	Bricklayer	T.P.Williams	C W	B W
Wakelin, Robert	Bricklayer	Clayton	C	B W
Wellicome, John	Plumber	T.P.Williams	C W	B W
Wellicome, Thomas	Plumber	Clayton	–	B W
Wigginton, Thomas	Coal Merchant	T.P.Williams	–	B W
Wigginton, William	Coal Merchant	T.P.Williams	C W	–
Wigginton, William	Grocer	Self	C	B W
Wright, Joseph	Paper Maker	Self	C	B W
Wright, William	Paper Maker	Self	C W	B W

to 2d., was admitted in 1845. He was Brangwyn's tenant
at Red Barn.

Name	Farm	Owner	1847	1852
Agar, Francis	Moor Farm	Clayton	–	B
Blackwell, Richard	Blunts Farm	Henry Micklem	C	B
Brangwyn, George	Barmoor	Self	C	B
Cheer, John	Town Farm	Dean & Chapter, Bristol	K W	K W
Corby, William	Munday Dean	Thomas Corby	–	K W
Crouch, William		T.P.Williams	K W	–
East, Joseph		Dean & Chapter, Bristol	C W	K W
Frost, Thomas	Hooks	Clayton	–	B W
Greenslade, Thomas	Homers	Mrs Rose	–	B
Keene, Alfred	Clay Lane	Joseph White	–	B
King, Richard	Widmere	Clayton	C	–
Oxlade, Thomas	Lane End	Self	K W	K W
Russell, Henry	Hawkins	Clayton	C	B
Simmonds, Joshua	Limmers	John Parker	C	K W
Wane, Isaac	Red Barn	George Brangwyn	C	B
Webb, Henry	Wymers	James Deane	C	–
Webb, James	Marlow Bottom	Ralph Harris	C	–

Another interesting sub-set of voters is provided by
the publicans:

Name	Ale-house	Owner	1847	1852
Abbot, G.	Greyhound, Spittal Street	Wethered	–	K W
Bowen, T.	Red Lion, West Street	Wethered	K W	K W
Brown, J.	Barge Pole, Church Passage	Alms House Trust	–	W
Brown, W.	Jolly Maltsters, Dean Street	John Griffiths	K W	B W
Cresswell, G.	Swan, Causeway	Wethered	K W	K W
Davis, D.	Chequers, High Street	T.P.Williams	K W	K W
Furnell, T.	Crown, Market Place	T.P.Williams	–	–
Hoare, C.	Three Horse Shoes, Gun Lane	T.P.Williams	C K	K W
Hobbs, J.	George & Dragon, Causeway	Wethered	K W	–
Meakes, H.	Cross Keys, Spittal Street	T.P.Williams	–	–
Neighbour, H.	Waterman, St Peter's Street	Gibbons	–	–
Plumridge, W.	White Hart, Chapel Street	T.P.Williams	K W	K W
Reeves, R.	Ship, West Street	T.P.Williams	–	K W
Sparks, W.	Black Boy, Church Passage	Wethered	K W	K W
Stephenson, J.	Coach & Horses, West Street	Clayton	C	B
Tyler, J.	Clayton Arms, Quoiting Place	Brakspear	–	–
White, Levi	Three Tuns, West Street	Wethered	K W	K W
Wyatt, G.	Horns, Chapel Street	Wethered	K W	K W

Predictably, almost all the votes were for the Tory candidates. Only John Stephenson, who lived in a house owned by Clayton, voted for the Liberal candidate in both elections. Charles Hoare, who split his vote in 1847, voted for Williams rather than Bell in 1852. Williams was his landlord, which may have influenced him.

The rest of the electorate voted for the Tory package. Williams came top of the poll in both the elections, which is not suprising when one considers how much influence he exerted in the town. It is perhaps difficult for us, for whom secret ballots are normal, to realise what it meant to have to sign the voting paper, so that it was clear what the choices had been, and then to have the lists printed so that everyone could read the results.

In addition to the borough's representation there were also members for Buckinghamshire. The franchise for voting for the county members was until 1832 the uniform qualification of being a forty shilling freeholder. This franchise continued after the Reform Act but was extended to cover all adult males possessed of copyhold land worth at least £10 a year and all adult males leasing or renting land worth at least £50 a year. Men in Great Marlow were in the Beaconsfield polling area and together with Wycombe made up the Hundred of Desborough. This Hundred, together with those of Burnham and Stoke, make up the Chiltern Hundreds, stewardship of which is still taken to vacate a seat in Parliament.

The County members at the time were Disraeli and Du Pre, Tories, and Cavendish, Whig and Gladstone was the Tory MP for the University of Oxford. Pressure and lobbying took place even at these levels and even bishops were not immune. Bishop Wilberforce wrote as follows:

> To the Rev. S B Arnott   Jan 18, 1853
> Most Confidential
> My dear Mr Arnott
>> I hear that your vote has not been given (ie promised) to Gladstone. I have myself the strongest convictions that the cause of the Church requires that it should be: and I cannot therefore forbear asking you to weigh the reasons which have convinced me and then acting as you see best.
>> Only keep this communication to yourself and burn it when read.

110

I am ever most truly yours,

S.Oxon.

Samuel Brazier Arnott lived at Court Gardens, Great Marlow, and was a St John's College man and so entitled to a University vote. According to the poll-book he was the last man to vote, but possibly he had considered the Bishop's views for he voted for Gladstone.

Sources

Davis, R.W., *Political Change and Continuity 1760-1885*, 1972.
Harris, J.R., *The Copper King*, 1964.
Copies of the poll for the Borough of Great Marlow for 31 July 1847 and 26 June 1852.

Agriculture

'Partly agricultural and partly manufacturing'

This was the conclusion of Thomas Rolls in 1840. He was treasurer of the feoffees, or governors, of Sir William Borlase's School, and was applying to the Ironmongers' Company for financial help for the school from Bettons Charity, which was administered by the Company. The quotation comes from his answer to a questionnaire in connection with this request and the description of Marlow applied equally well in 1851. Indeed, agriculture did not play as important a role in the economic life of the parish of Great Marlow in mid-Victorian times as it did generally in the county of Buckinghamshire or in the country as a whole. This can be seen from the following table:

	England	Bucks	Marlow
Agricultural workers as percentage of male population	21.7	33	9

These figures include farmers, their sons, and farmworkers of all categories, but not wives and daughters though they must have contributed much labour in both house and field. Nevertheless a significant proportion of the population of the parish was directly or indirectly associated with farming. Many of the town-dwellers owned or rented fields in and around the town or in the strip system of the common fields. Horses were kept, of course, and often a few cows, but the owners had other main occupations. Thomas Gibbons, who lived in St Peter's Street, appears in the Directory as farmer and also coal merchant, and James Bird Brooks, of the Causeway, is listed as farmer, baker, and corn, flour and hay dealer. The Rate Book describes his property as a house and yard. Town dairies were a feature of this period and were to continue into the next century. Many people had cows within the town, often entirely stall-kept, and supplied milk to the neighbouring townspeople. James Cox, for example, who lived in Spittal Street, is described as a cow-keeper in the Directory; in the census returns he is recorded as a farmer of thirty-five acres employing three labourers.

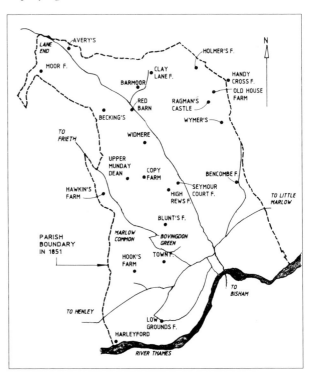

Map to show the position of farms mentioned in the 1851 census. At that time most of the farmers were tenants; George Brangwyn at Barmoor and William Gaskell at Lane End were exceptional in being owner-occupiers. Drawn by Joan Rogers

In the mid-nineteenth century the majority of the farms in the parish belonged to large estates – the major landowners being the University of Oxford, the Dean and Chapter of Bristol and the Clayton family who had lived at Harleyford since 1735. Their estate ranged from Harleyford itself in the west to Lane End in the north and they also owned a considerable number of strips in the common fields. In addition the Dean and Chapter of Gloucester also owned property in the town of Marlow and land in the strip system to the south and west of the

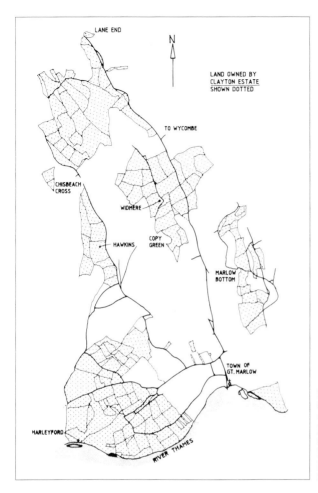

Map of the Harleyford estate
showing that Sir William
Clayton owned Moor Farm,
Hawkins, Hooks, Widmere
and Marlow Bottom. Drawn
by Joan Rogers from a
photograph of the original
map

town. There were various other landlords with smaller
properties, such as James Deane who owned Wymers and
Ragman's Castle, Joseph White who owned Clay Lane,
Mrs Rose at Holmers and the Hammond family who
owned a farm at Copy Green. In the nineteenth century,
many of the farmers worked fields that were not arranged
together to form a compact holding. The scattered fields
of the Hammond family at Copy Farm may be contrasted
with the almost ideal plan at Widmere where the fields
were arranged around the central farmhouse.

115

Very few farmers both owned and worked their own farms. The voters' list for the Beaconsfield district for 1851, of which Marlow was a part for the purposes of county elections, lists those entitled to vote. Electors had to be freeholders and, apart from local landowners, only two names out of those listed in the 1851 census returns as farmers appear – George Brangwyn of Barmoor and William Gaskell of Lane End.

In Buckinghamshire as a whole tenancies in the nineteenth century were usually on a yearly basis, with six months' notice, and so there was little incentive for farmers to improve the ground. In Marlow, however, the Harleyford Estate accounts show that the Claytons granted leases of up to fourteen years with few penalties, except in the last three years. Most landlords extracted fines from tenants who sold hay or straw off the land or who ploughed up pasture. These penalties were mentioned by the Reverend St John Priest in 1813, together with the comment that tenants were often prepared to pay the fines for ploughing up pasture because 'the growers of woad will give great price for sward newly broken from grass',apparently as much as six to eight guineas an acre.

Common Fields

In addition to the large estates and farms, mid-nineteenth-century Marlow parish retained the remnants of the 'strip system' of farming to the south-east and north-east of the town, as can be seen from the Tithe Apportionment map of 1843. The strips were small areas of ground, often of less than an acre, arranged mostly in parallel and usually in multiples of one chain wide and one furlong long. They belonged to various owners and were worked by varying tenants, many of whom had grazing and other rights over the whole area. Many of the strips in the common fields were leased by the Dean and Chapter of Bristol to Owen and William Wethered or to William Creswell for terms of twenty-one years from 29 September 1851 and 1852. Similarly strips owned by the Dean and Chapter of Gloucester were leased for twenty-one years to George Cannon from 29 September 1852 and to William and Joseph Wright from 29

September 1850. These long leases were unusual for their time and may perhaps have reflected ecclesiastical estate policy.

The Rate Books refer to the Great Common Field, the Eastern Field, West Field and Marefield. Most of the ground is described on the tithe map as arable and a great deal of it must have been subject to flooding. Within living memory cattle grazing in the Gossmore area have had to be swum out in time of flood. Working strips can hardly have been an ideal way of farming and at least one critic of the system wrote 'Anyone who wishes to see the horrors of open lands should visit Great Marlow Field.'

Tithes

Payment of tithes to the church, either in kind or in money, was a survival from times when agriculture was the main occupation of the people. Tithes were the tenth part of the main produce of the land, such as corn, oats and wood,and the tenth part of the produce of both stock and labour, such as wool, pigs and milk. They were paid to the local church. The person holding the rectorship of the parish might or might not be the incumbent as well. If not then he had the right, subject to the bishop of the diocese, to appoint a vicar to look after the souls of the parishioners. If that happened then the rector usually took the great tithes, easily collected valuable items, and the vicar was left with the small tithes, deriving from minor produce and labour. The system was resented by the Victorian farming community, as by their successors, and considered an unfair burden, particularly as no such tax was levied on the products of factories. Edward Sawyer of Great Marlow had already made this abundantly clear in a letter of 24 July 1830:

> *To the Most Reverend Father of the Church of England Archbishop of Canterbury*
> *....There is many unpleasant things happen in taking the tithes in kind after the farmer have done his best for his crop to have the tenth taken by the Rector or the Layman as taking the tithes is the greatest evil in the country....*
> *....As I am plain John Bull knows more about*

117

farming than I do about Grammar'

The Marlow tithes were the subject of much dispute both before and after they were commuted to payment in money under the terms of the Tithe Commutation Act of 1836. In the early part of the nineteenth century the tithes of the parish of Great Marlow were owned by the Dean and Chapter of Gloucester and were divided into two halves, according to local custom. The two halves were exchanged periodically to maintain fairness. In 1843, the date of the Tithe Apportionment map, one half was let to Mary Wright, whose husband had previously held the lease – the Wrights had paper mills in Marlow. The other eastern half was let to James Deane, who lived in Tunbridge Wells and who sub-let it to Henry Webb, his tenant at High Rews farm in the parish. Henry Webb received his share partly in kind and partly in money, but Mary Wright received her share in cash. She died in 1850 and the 1852 Church Rate Book shows her tithing inherited by four people:

John Morgan	who was married to a Wright
William Greenwood	really on behalf of his daughter who was a Wright grandchild
William Wright	
.Joseph Wright	

Reference to the will of Mary Wright's husband, Joseph senior, who died in 1836, suggests that the later apportionment of Mary's half-tithe was not quite as he had intended, but the Morgans and the Wrights remained on good terms despite disputes.

The Tithe Apportionment map of 1843 was drawn up in detail for the whole of the parish. Its purpose was to show who owned and who 'occupied' or worked each field or portion of land so that the tithes of the parish might be accurately assessed and the details provided about the farms and fields are invaluable for local historians.

At the time of the tithe map almost the whole of the parish farmland – apart from the established woodland, which remains unchanged to this day – was under arable cultivation. The area was part of the great local granary for London. The only permanent grasslands were the river

Barn at High Rews Farm, 1991. Drawn by Margaret Richardson

meadows along the Thames and the parkland around Seymour Court. The use of the term 'arable' is open to wide interpretation; considerable amounts of hay must have been grown to feed the horses and most of the farmers seem to have employed a long rotation with sainfoin, clover and seeds hay being grown for several years on what was termed arable ground.

John Rolfe made the estimates of the average cropping and evaluation of the Great and Small Tithes of the parish in 1840. He was a land surveyor from Beaconsfield and had previously surveyed the area in 1833/34 in connection with a re-assessment of the poor rate in the parish. He divided the arable land into four classes, giving estimated values for crops of turnips, barley, clover, wheat and oats, after allowing for expenses of harvesting, thatching and so on. Meadow land was divided into three classes. He found that the acreage of the lands in the parish which were subject to the payment of tithes amounted to just over 6,107 acres, of which about 4,256 acres were arable. In south Buckinghamshire, according to local custom, beechwood was exempt from tithe. Rolfe commented that the value of Marlow's Great Tithe produce in wheat, barley and oats was greatly lowered by being mixed 'all sorts and qualities together' so that it could not go for seed nor for the best flour nor for malting but had to be sold as seconds. The same description applied to hay. When the Tithe Commission's Award for Marlow was finally published in April 1841, Rolfe's estimate had been accepted but not his suggestion of a five per cent reduction in the value of the produce because of the mixed quality.

Enclosures

The enclosure of the common fields of Great Marlow was late in comparison with the rest of the country – the Award was made in 1855, following Acts in 1845 and 1852. A copy of the Award made for the Wethered family is dated as 'confirmed' on 13 September 1858, and shows Richard Hall of Delahay Street, Westminster, to have been appointed as Valuer. After all the objections had been heard Mr Hall listed his awards. He also listed in detail those public roads and footpaths which he had 'stopped up' and the names of the people who were to be responsible for the fencing and maintenance of the boundary of each piece of land which he had sold to defray the expenses incidental to the enclosure. In addition some parcels of land were to be exchanged. It is particularly interesting that the valuer did 'set out, allot and award' five acres of land, identified as the area numbered 40 on the map, to the churchwardens and overseers in trust as a place for exercise and recreation for the inhabitants of the parish. This field near Gossmore is still in use today as a recreation ground.

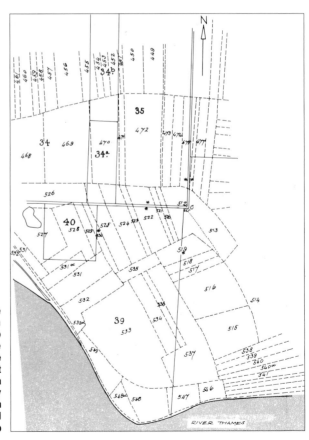

Map showing part of the common field system from the Tithe Apportionment map of 1843 overlain by the boundaries of the Enclosure Award. The rectangular plot numbered 40 is still a recreation ground. Drawn by Joan Rogers from photographs of the original map

Farming practice

According to the census returns twenty-one men gave their occupation as that of farmer. Ten were born in Marlow and the majority of the others were local men. Rents at the time were just over £1 per acre and some idea of the likely costs of tenancies can be gained from the following table showing the acreages of farms; the number of labourers is also shown.

Farm Tenancies and Acreages in 1851			
Farmer	**Farm**	**Acreage**	**No of workers**
Owen Wethered	Various	417	24 men, 5 women 10 boys, 1 son
Sarah & Thomas King	Widmere	340	15
George Brangwyn	Barmoor	230	12
John Curtis	Lowgrounds	230	7, 1 son
William Corby	Munday Dean	210	10
Thomas Frost	Hooks	190	4
John Miller	Marlow Bottom	162	12, 1 son
Henry Russell	Hawkins	140	7
Alfred Keene	Clay Lane	127	5
Thomas Greenslade	Holmers	120	5
James Taylor	Becking (Beacon)	109	2
James Franklin	Prospect House	100	5
Joshua Simmonds	Limmers	98	5
Isaac Wane	Red Barn	65	2
William Gaskell	Lane End (Cutlers?)	56	3, 1 son
Henry Webb	Wymers	56	3, 1 son
William Creswell	Wycombe Road	52	?
James Cox	Spittal Street	35	3, 1 son
William Crouch	Spittal Street	12	2, 1 son
Sydney Gibbons	Seymours	?	?
Oxlade	Lane End (?Moor farm)	?	?

On average the farmers of 1851 employed one man for every 22 acres and many lived-in on the farm. The census returns show that many of them were unmarried, even those aged forty or fifty, and the practice of living-in was slow to die out. Young men were still living-in at Widmere in the 1930s.

The Wethered wages books for 1843 show that a skilled man, such as a ploughman, carter or shepherd, could earn 12s. to 13s. a week, with boys earning 4s. or 4s.6d.. This level remained unchanged until 1865 when ploughmen received 15s. and shepherds 14s. Wages could therefore cost the farmers of 1851 about £40 a year for a skilled worker and even if only half the labourers were paid at this rate and the remainder at £20 a year the bill for wages would still add another £1.10s. per acre to the farmer's costs. An expenditure of £2.10s. per acre on rent and wages, together with the cost of seed and any bought 'fertiliser', tithes, rates and taxes would leave little margin for profit if John Rolfe's valuations of 1840 still held true. He showed a titheable return of £4.9s. per acre for first class arable land, £3.6s.4d. per acre for second class and down to as low as £2.10s.4d. for fourth class after allowing for harvest expenses. Lower values were shown for sainfoin and meadowland.

The Wethereds employed men in their brewery as well as on their farms and it is interesting to try to compare the wage levels in both kinds of work. One of the obvious difficulties is that it is difficult to know which jobs to set side by side; another is that the brewery wages sheets which we studied are for 1858, whereas the farm wages are for 1850. Nevertheless the following figures serve to give some idea:

Farm and Brewery workers' wages per week			
	Farm 1850		**Brewery 1858**
Bailiff	21s.	**Cooper**	20s.
		Carpenter	18s.
		Engineer	18s.
		Drayman	14s.-18s.
		Tinman	17s.6d.
Shepherd	13s.	**Chaff Cutters**	12s.-13s.6d.
		Helpers	8s.8d.-12s.6d.
Ploughman	12s.		
Milkman	12s.		
Carter	12s.		
Boys	4s.-5s.		

In order to get some idea of the relative value of these wage figures it is necessary to know what prices were like in the 1850s. At that time the currency was old pennies, 240 of them making up a pound, but the following examples should help.

Product	Quantity	Price in old pennies
Milk	2 pints	1
Eggs	a dozen	5
Butter	2lbs.	11
Beer	a gallon	5
Bread	4lb. loaf	3½
Beef	1lb.	3
Pork	1lb.	4
Bacon	1lb.	5
Potatoes	14lbs.	2
Tea	2lbs.	33
Coffee	1lb.	5
Coal	a ton	86
Railway travel	a mile	1

The census returns show that 221 people, two of whom were women, gave their occupation as farm labourer, with ages ranging from eight to ninety-two. The discrepancy between these figures and the numbers listed as employed by farmers can perhaps be partly explained by the fact that some of the work was seasonal and the census date of the end of March was not at a peak time in the agricultural year. Also many of the men were likely to have worked on farms which were nearby but not within the parish such as Handy Cross and the farms in Little Marlow. Most of the farm workers were born in Marlow as were their wives and many of them lived in Dean Street. Unfortunately their place of work is not usually given.

The returns also show that there were at the time at least four bailiffs or stewards who were farming directly for landowners or the chief tenants. These were men with responsibility and were paid considerably more than the farm workers although still on a weekly basis. For example John Cheer lived at Town Farm, which was owned by his employer, Thomas Wethered, and earned 21s. a week in 1857, a wage which remained unchanged for the various bailiffs working for the Wethereds up until 1880. Incidentally, three of John Cheer's daughters were married in Marlow Church on the same day, 23 April 1873. There was much celebration in the town – 'Three Cheers' indeed.

Accounts of farm sales give an insight into both the stock and the practices at the time. The Kings had been tenant farmers at Burford Farm, Marlow Bottom, as well as at Widmere, but Richard King died between 1847 and 1851 and so his widow Sarah sold the stock at Burford Farm. The notice of the auction, to be conducted by Messrs. Rolls of Great Marlow, appeared in the *Windsor and Eton Express* for 17 May 1851.

Sales by Auction
Burford Farm, Great Marlow
TO BE SOLD BY AUCTION
By Messrs.ROLLS,
On MONDAY, May 19th, 1851, at Twelve o'clock,
On the Premises, by the direction of Mrs. King, who is leaving the above farm, all the valuable
LIVE and DEAD FARMING STOCK, Two Ricks of fine Wheat, Implements in Husbandry, etc.; comprising 2 three-year old, and 3 two-year old Colts, and 2 Yearlings, 3 light market wagons, ! ditto nearly new, 4 strong dung carts, grass cart and a market cart, 4 horse thrashing machine in good working order, 4 nine stone rick saddles with caps and timbers, winnowing and blowing machines, 2 turnip and ash drills, 1 pea ditto, 4 scarifiers, 3 two-wheel ploughs, 6 pairs of strong four and five-beam harrows, 3 cast iron pig troughs, 2 sets of harness with collars and bit halters, 40 round ladder, quantity of old Iron, and a well-built dark-bodied gig, etc..

Although Hambleden is outside the parish, the following notice of the sale of Mill End Farm is included, partly because Thomas Brangevin was probably a relative, perhaps a brother, of George Brangwyn, and also because the details of the brewing stock are interesting. Again Messrs. Rolls were the auctioneers and the notice appeared in the *Windsor and Eton Express* for 27 September 1851.

HAMBLEDEN, BUCKS,
MILL END FARM, between HENLEY and MARLOW.

MESSRS. ROLLS are directed by Mr. Thomas Brangwin, who is leaving, to SELL by AUCTION, on MONDAY, October 6th, 1851, on the Premises, at Eleven o'clock, the valuable LIVE and DEAD FARMING STOCK, Agricultural Implements, and a capital seasoned Brewing Plant, including a 200-gallon copper, 10-bushel iron bound mash tub, fir coolers, 7 72 and 2 36-gallon casks, &c. The capital Stock comprises 4 handsome short-horn in-calf cows, 2 barren cows, 6 three-year-old fat heifers (fit for the butcher), 3 calves and a three-year-old short-horned bull, 3 useful cart horses, 2 bay hackneys and an excellent 4-year-old harness mare, by Mr. Hussey's well known horse Cowl, 16 store pigs, 2 young in-pig sows and a young boar pig, 4 capital 9-stone rick staddles with caps and oak timbers, a strong, well constructed, double shaff waggon, with iron arms and ladders in good preservation, a light well-built spring cart, and a pony gig; grass-sowing, hay-making, and winnowing machines, Suffolk drills, turnip drills, 2 capital malt mills, water barrel and frame, a gin with monkey for driving piles, 3 cast-iron pig troughs, barn implements, &c., &c.

May be viewed on Saturday preceding the sale, and catalogues had at the market inns in Henley, Maidenhead, and Wycombe; at the Red Lion, Nettlebed; Hare and Hounds, Hambleden; and at the farm of Messrs. Rolls, Marlow.

Root drill, supplied by Battings of Marlow and still used in 1991. Reproduced by courtesy of G.J. White, Widmere Farm

Trapped between landlord and labourer and encumbered with church rates, tithes and taxes – even on dogs and horses – the mid-nineteenth-century farmers had much to contend with. They were the focus of much rural discontent and, as now, were subject to vehement criticism by town dwellers. A letter to *The Times* in 1851 quotes a menu for a lavish farmers' dinner and maintains that cries of 'ruinous times' from the farmers must be viewed with scepticism. In some ways, however, this was an exciting period with many new ideas about crops and rotations and the development of new agricultural machines. The introduction of new methods and other innovations were not always readily accepted by the farmers of the time – then, as now, a conservative body. The same issue of *The Times* in 1851 printed a long report of the speeches at a dinner of the Surrey Agricultural Association in which several speakers doubted the value of science to agriculture and urged practical advances only. Even the value of the mechanical reaper, newly introduced in 1851, was thought by one speaker to be doubtful as very little labour would be saved. Corn still

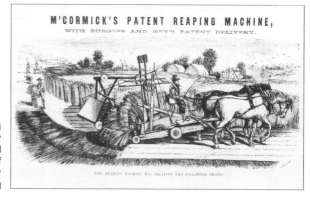

M'Cormick's patent reaping machine. Print supplied by the Institute of Agricultural History and Museum of English Rural Life, University of Reading

had to be bound by hand – the miracle of the mechanical binder was yet to come.

As history was to show, the farmers of 1851 were in fact living in what was a 'high farming' period, but crop prices were already showing signs of the coming depression. The average selling price of wheat in 1851 was the lowest for the century so far. Later, in the 1870s, as transport improved (the railway reached Marlow in 1873), imported food became cheap throughout the country and there began a period of severe decline in the agriculture of this and most other areas – a depression so severe indeed that by the turn of the century many of the farms were without tenants. Many were taken 'in hand' by the landowners and some became derelict for a time. As the new century progressed several of the farms became gradually eroded by housing estates (Marlow Bottom, Limmers, Holmers) and one even became a small airfield (Barmoor). Some of the farms survived, however, and Widmere and High Rews are two examples. Work on the hedges of these two farms showed that almost all of them were considerably over two hundred years old and this is confirmed by a comparative study of the plans of the fields in the 1843 tithe map and the same fields in modern farm maps. The field shapes and boundaries are more or less identical and the hedges have largely been retained in this district of gentle hills and valleys. Many aspects of life on Marlow farms have changed beyond recognition in the past 150 years but there is some reassurance in the continuity of hedgerows. Many of them have been there since medieval times – will they be there in a hundred years' time?

Stables at High Rews Farm, 1991. Drawn by Margaret Richardson

Stable at Widmere Farm, 1991. Drawn by Margaret Richardson

The chapel at Widmere Farm in 1905. Built in the thirteenth century, it overlies an earlier Norman crypt; the chapel was used as living quarters for farm labourers in the nineteenth century. Reproduced by courtesy of the Royal Commission on the Historical Monuments of England

Shorthorn calves at Widmere

127

Sources

Chambers J.D. and Mingay G.E., *The Agricultural Revolution 1750/1880*, 1966.
Priest, St.J., *General View of Agriculture in Buckinghamshire*, 1813.
Reed, C.S., 'Agriculture in Buckinghamshire', *Journal of the Royal Agricultural Society of England* 16 (1855), 269.
John Rolfe, *Valuation of Great Marlow Tithes 1840/1*, Public Record Office IR29/3/75.
Edward Sawyer's letter, Buckinghamshire Record Office D/LE/14/37.

The Church and the Vestry

The church played a very important role in the running of Marlow in the mid-nineteenth century, in that most of the local government functions were carried out by the parish vestry, which also looked after the affairs of the church. The two sets of functions were, however, minuted separately and, in the case of many of the secular functions, some of the records have not been found. Originally vestries were entirely ecclesiastical organisations, consisting of a meeting together of parishioners to discuss church business. From the sixteenth century onwards the hundred and manorial courts, which had dealt with more secular matters, began to decline. Hundred courts started in the tenth century and served areas of administration which were larger than parishes but smaller than shires or counties; manorial courts were related to manors. The vestry was the natural successor to both of them. It was able to impose a church rate, the original purpose of which was for the repair and maintenance of the church fabric, and gradually acquired other powers principally for supporting the poor as well as for looking after highways and collecting taxes.

The dates of some vestry meetings were fixed in accordance with certain church canons or acts of parliament. For example, the meeting to elect the churchwardens had to be held at Easter, and the meeting to choose the overseers had to be 'in Easter week or within one month after Easter'. By the Parish Constables Act of 1842 it was laid down that the vestry meeting to nominate the constables, quite important figures of authority in the parish, should be held between 27 February and 24 March each year.

In 1850 the vicar of Great Marlow parish was the Reverend Thomas Tracey Coxwell. The parish, formerly in Lincoln diocese, was transferred to the Diocese of Oxford in 1845 and in the following year the bishop, Samuel Wilberforce, wrote to Mr Coxwell:

> *Cuddesdon Palace, Feb 10 1846,*
> *address me at 61 Eaton Place*
> To the Rev.T.T.Coxwell
>
> *Rev. Sir*
> *I am led to address you by the accounts which from various sources I have received of the State of the Parish of Great Marlow, committed by God's Providence to your Care and Government,*
> I   *I find that you have only one Sermon in your church on Sunday*
> II   *That from your own age it is impossible for you to give the daily, hourly, attention which such a parish needs; and*
> III *That you have no resident curate.*
> *I beg therefore, Rev. Sir, in the Name of Christ and for the sake of His Church, and in remembrance of that strict and fearful account which we shall both render before His Judgement Seat, to exhort and beseech you to set yourself immediately to the due ordering of these matters.*
> *I am Rev. Sir, your faithful friend and brother,*
> *S.Oxon.*

The bishop noted in his Diocese Book that Coxwell was a 'very old man' – he was sixty-five at the time – and that he had not given adequate time for candidates to prepare themselves for confirmation. The vicar must have written back about the church's financial situation because the bishop's next letter, written on 18 February, read:

> *I can of course quite enter into your difficulty as to providing an assistant from so small an endowment. Still the **first** necessity of all, for yourself as well as for them, is that the souls committed to you should be so cared for as that you may render your account with joy in **that** day – and I hope that this matter may be arranged if as I understand you are willing to put it into my hands. But upon this point we should be quite clear. Do I then understand that you desire me to nominate an assistant curate for Great Marlow provided his salary is secured without charge to yourself.*
> *I am, Rev. Sir, Very sincerely yours,*
> *S.Oxon.*

According to Slaters Directory for 1851 the sum of £2,560 16s. 6d. had been subscribed for a curacy, headed by a donation of £1,000 from Thomas Wethered, who died in 1849, so the bishop was as good as his word. This was a period of vigorous reform in the Church of England and it is interesting to see the very direct effect this could have on individual localities. Wilberforce was an active and forceful bishop and his action to improve the performance of the church in Great Marlow was a small part of the general movement at the time.

All Saints Church had been rebuilt between 1832 and 1835. The earlier church had been subject to flooding ever since the first pound lock had been built at Marlow in 1773. In 1809, for instance, the water was said to have risen 'over the third step as you go up into the singing gallery'. When the new pound lock was built in 1825 the effect was to raise the water-level upstream, thereby increasing the likelihood of flooding still further. A survey was made of the old church in 1830 which records water-marks on the pews 'about 17 inches' above the floor of the church.

> The mischievous consequences of such a state of the Building to the health of the Parties attending worship therein, as well as the injurious effect to the fabric, which is extensively cover'd with a green vegetation, are such as to call loudly for an amendment in that particular.

The tower and spire of this church fell in 1831 and the new building on the same site was consecrated in 1835. The main contractor was William Bond of Great Marlow, who was also concerned with the new bridge, built at virtually the same time.

In 1851 the church in its commanding position at the end of High Street and close to the newly-sited suspension bridge, would have consisted of a rectangular brick nave with three high, gaunt-looking entrances at the west end surmounted by a small tower and spire. The chancel was added in 1875-76, arcades were inserted, the tower was remodelled and the 1832 windows were replaced by ones with elaborate Gothic tracery.

The money to pay for the rebuilding of All Saints Church had been raised as a loan. The cost had been

Interior of All Saints Church in 1877, but looking much as it must have done in 1851 with galleries and box pews. Reproduced by courtesy of the Royal Commission on the Historical Monuments of England

£15,654 and the money was being paid back, over the years, by the parishioners. Each year a meeting was held in midsummer to fix the rate of repayment for the coming year and everyone, except those who were on poor relief of some kind, had to pay.

Sir William Clayton, who lived at Harleyford, was one of the Trustees and his correspondence on the matter makes interesting reading. When he received notification of the date of the meeting to fix the rate for 1851/52 he wrote:

> *79 Gloucester Place*
> *Portman Square*
> *June 23^{d}*
>
> *Sir*
> *I regret to find that the Meeting of the General Trustees, under the Marlow Church Building Act, is again appointed, at a most inconvenient period of the Year, when our engagements call us elsewhere – few efficient General Trustees remain– Much dissatisfaction exists, among the church building Rate payers, as to the amount of Rates now for long levied upon the Parish. It is quite clear either, that a reduction in the am^{t} of Rate to be paid **sh^{d} take place, or, that a**

132

*very clear and **categorical acc^t should** be placed before the Church Building Genl Trustees for their guidance and information.*

*I am aware of the extraordinary clause in the Act, liberating from responsibility; – but, **honest** men should not, and must not, take umbrage accordingly –*

*These are points, which in my opinion, should be seriously considered, and **well** weighed at the next meeting on the 26th – It is **im**possible that I can attend, as I am **obliged** to be at Woolwich on **that** day*

> *Your most obedient s^{nt}*
> *William Rob: Clayton*

According to the Secretary of the Trustees, William Lakin Ward, solicitor, Sir William's letter was put before the other Trustees when they met on 26 June. The meeting was attended by the new vicar Frederick Bussell, Mr Coxwell having retired, Thomas Rolls, Owen Wethered, Alex Higginson, Robert Maddocks, George Cannon and Robert Hammond – a very representative gathering of the men who ran the affairs of Great Marlow at the time. We cannot be sure which Thomas Rolls this was, but it seems likely that he was the same one who was treasurer of the governors of the Free School, in which case it was, as the records say, 'Mr Rolls (Bridge)'. Higginson and Hammond played less part in the vestry affairs than the others but, listed as they were in the directories as gentry, this is not suprising.

The rate was fixed at one shilling in the pound, an increase of twopence on the previous year. Sir William did not let this pass without comment as the following extract of his next letter, dated 27 June 1851, shows:

*The Magistrates no doubt with excellent judgement and in their discretion, excuse Rates – But why the people are to be heavily taxed beyond that which the act contemplated and empowered I know not – 75$^£$ is a serious sum – and **Arrears not** excused by Magistrates **should be collected** – at least, every legal measure shd be adopted to recover them, (the Arrears) before the Committee laid a **further** tax on the Ratepayer to make good the deficiency – The sum ought not to be allowed to the outgoing Churchwardens without some*

133

*strict investigation – and depend upon it, we as a Committee are wrong, in taxing further, the people, until we can show a better case than at present – 75$^£$ loss on the Church Rate is a fearful sacrifice – it is nearly 3^d in the pound upon a rating of **540$^£$** – and would nearly pay the interests of two **1,000$^£$** Bonds at 4 p^{r}C^t the amount of interest now paid to the holders of the Marlow **New** Church Bonds*

*I am one of many others who pay a **very** heavy rate – as a landed proprietor*

As well as repaying the loan on the church the parishioners had to provide the churchwardens with money each year to pay the bills. These included the costs of cleaning, playing the organ, providing the communion wine, and keeping the churchyard tidy, as well as paying the parish clerk. Churchwardens were elected each year and their accounts were presented to a meeting of the vestry, usually in October.

In 1851 the meeting to elect the churchwardens for Great Marlow was held on 22 April. The vestry usually met in the National School Room in Quoiting Place and the minutes of this meeting state:

Great Marlow Bucks April 22nd 1851

At a meeting of the inhabitants of this parish in Vestry assembled this day at the National School Room pursuant to a notice given on the Church Doors on the Two Sundays preceding as well as being according to the usual custom (being Easter Tuesday) for the appointment of Two Churchwardens for the said Parish of Great Marlow in the County of Buckingham We, whose names are hereunder subscribed have chosen the Two Persons, whose names are hereunder written to be the Churchwardens for this Parish for the year ensuing.

> *Robert Maddocks Churchwarden for the Vicar*
>
> *Fr. Bussell, Vicar*
> *George Cannon Churchwarden for the Parish*
>
>> *Inhabitants*
>> *Owen Wethered*
>> *Thomas Gibbons*
>> *John Gibbons*
>> *Ralph Spicer*

Thomas Rolls
William Ward
Henry Stallwood
L.W.Wethered.

Some of these names are familiar by now. Both the Wethered sons were there, Mr Ward the solicitor and Thomas Rolls from the bridge. Thomas Gibbons was the coal merchant in St Peter's Street and John Gibbons was a grocer and tallow-chandler in West Street. Ralph Spicer was a solicitor, also from West Street, and Henry Stallwood lived in Chapel Street.

The accounts for the previous twelve months were approved at the vestry meeting on 10 October 1851 and a fortnight later, on 24 October, a meeting was called 'to make a Church Rate for the necessary expences of the Church, and also to take into consideration the propriety of augmenting the salaries of the several officers attending the extra duties of the church'.

Robert Maddocks and George Cannon explained that they would need a rate of threepence in the pound and Mr Maddocks formally proposed this. It was seconded by Thomas Rolls. Isaac Wane,a young farmer from Red Barn Farm, proposed a rate of twopence, as an amendment, and this was seconded by Stephen Shoosmith. One can speculate on whether Mr Wane was against paying a higher than necessary rate anyway or whether there was a difference of opinion between town-livers and those living in the outer parish, the latter possibly unwilling to pay for what they saw as essentially a 'town' service. It is also the case that farm land was highly rated, as Clayton had pointed out; Isaac Wane's land was assessed at £52 14s. in 1851, which meant that his contribution to the rebuilding of the church, at a shilling in the pound, was £2 12s.9d. and for the church rates £1 5s. 6d., whereas Robert Maddocks was paying 10s.4d. and 3s. respectively. The minutes say that the Chairman, who was the vicar, thought that, on a division, 'the Majority present was in favour of the Rate at Twopence in the Pound'. Thereupon the churchwardens demanded a poll, which was agreed. It was held the same day until four o'clock and the following day from ten until four. In spite of what we might think of as rather short notice 163 people voted, the final count being 98 for a 3d. rate and 65 for a 2d. rate, a majority of 33 for the higher rate.

So Cannon and Maddocks had an income of £130.3s.10d. to cover church expenses for the year, made up of £2.18s.4d. left over from the previous year as balance in hand and the rest resulting from the agreed 3d. rate. Their expenditure is all set out in the accounts and makes interesting reading. The bishop made his triennial visitation that year and they had to pay £2.5s.8d. fees and £2.14s.8d. expenses, not to mention paying the bell-ringers £1.1s.. 'Blowing the organ' cost the parish 10s.6d. a quarter while the organist, Henry Badger, was paid £6.0s.every six months. He was also the parish clerk and was paid £5.0s. each half-year for that. William Truss was the church cleaner and earned £1.10s. every three months, though he got an extra ten shillings for six months' gardening. David Davis, who kept the Chequers, provided the sacramental wine on at least two occasions and Robert Foottit was paid for wax candles. It is noticeable that, wherever possible, the churchwardens seem to have used a variety of suppliers in the town, presumably to avoid any suggestion of favouritism or special deals. An unusual item was 'A large Prayer Book Morocco Elegant for Reading Desk, ordered by the Rural Dean' which cost £6.10s.. The accounts end at the end of April 1852 and they had spent £127.19s.8d.. Rates excused were given as 16s. so they ended their year with a balance of £1.8s.1d. to hand on.

The secular meetings of the vestry were concerned with day-to-day administration of the town and were responsible for nominating or appointing local people to look after Great Marlow's affairs. In February 1851 Robert Maddocks chaired a meeting of the vestry to nominate men for the job of constable and as assessors of taxes. The list of nominations for constable, normally twenty-four names, was sent to the magistrates at petty sessions for a decision as to who should be appointed. The 1842 Act stated that constables should be aged between 25 and 55, and they also had to be paying more than £4 a year in rent. There were usually two constables in any one year but three men seem to have held this office, not, apparently, a popular one, in 1851. They were John Smith, the china dealer in High Street, Thomas Walker who lived in Market

Street and William Davis. There are three men called William Davis in the census returns, a painter's labourer in Chapel Street, a fruiterer in Gun Lane and a carpenter's labourer in Spittal Street. Of these, William Davis of Chapel Street seems the most likely on the basis of his annual rent. The evidence for Smith comes from the churchwardens' accounts, where the entry for 21 April 1851 reads:

> *Paid John Smith (constable) as per Bill £1.3.0.*

Thomas Walker features more than once in the newspaper reports of petty sessions and in the following case both he and Davis are mentioned. The case, reported first on 1 March 1851, came up at the Lent Assizes on 15 March and was written up:

> *Henry Robinson and George Rymel were charged with selling two pieces of wood, the property of Mr Creswell of Great Marlow. William Davis proved finding the property in the possession of the prisoners. Mr J Creswell – I am a farmer of Great Marlow; from information received from Walker, a constable, I missed two pieces of wood, which wood I afterwards saw in the care of Davis the constable. Thomas Walker – I am a constable at Marlow; on the evening of 25th February last, I saw Robinson with a piece of wood; I took him into custody, and found that the wood had been stolen from Mr Creswell; Reymell has the other piece of wood.*
>
> *Prisoners in defence stated that they found the two pieces of wood, and were about carrying them home when the constable came up to them.*

They were found guilty and Reymell, who had been convicted before, was sentenced to a year's hard labour and Robinson to two months.

The role of the men who were elected as assessors was to assess the inhabitants for the poor rate and to see that it was collected. Twelve men were nominated for this office at the February meeting:

For the Town	For the Parish
William Bond, builder	John Curtis, farmer, Low Grounds
Josiah Clark, grocer	Ralph Rose, proprietor of houses
James Lovegrove, plumber	Joshua Simmonds, farmer, Limmers
Edward Hewett, draper	George Brangwyn, farmer, Barmoor
William Westbrook, butcher	William Wright, paper manufacturer
John Morgan, draper	William Jaques, corn miller

The vestry also appointed annually the Surveyor of Highways who, at the time we are interested in, was always Thomas Bowen. His annual salary was £25 and he was also the landlord of the Red Lion in West Street. He was born in Marlow in 1800 and lived with his wife. His account book for 1852/3 survives; it was the 27th edition of a book called:

Johnson's Surveyor of the Highways' Account Book
drawn agreeably to the Act 5 & 6 Wm.IV Cap.50
by William Richardson,
District Surveyor of the Parish of Charlton, Kent.

The author wrote the book 'to assist fellow surveyors in keeping the accounts, he having previously found the method hitherto adopted to be ill-arranged, defective and totally inadequate for keeping a proper and correct account'. The book contains information and suggestions for the repairing of 'old Roads' and pages of extraordinarily complicated and extensive headings under which the surveyor was supposed to enter his records and figures. Thomas Bowen did not complete his book very comprehensively, but his accounts were presented to the vestry meeting on 26 March 1853 and verified by two of Her Majesty's Justices of the Peace for the County of Buckinghamshire at 'a special session for the Highways, holden at the Crown Inn in Great Marlow in the County of Bucks the second day of April 1853'. Thomas Bowen was nominated and appointed again as Surveyor so his records must have been satisfactory.

Another concern of the vestry was that of gas lighting. This was provided by the Great Marlow Gas Company, which was established in 1845. The gas works were in Marefield Passage and the superintendent was Henry Salmon, who is also said to have been an proved by the Bible,

Mr. Atkinson also challenges Dr. Cahall, or an other priest or layman, to discussion on these subject

1848. GREAT MARLOW. *Oct. 21*

At a meeting of the rate-payers held on the 16th inst., it was determined to adopt so much of the Act of 3rd and 4th Wm. 4th, as respects the Lighting of the town of Great Marlow. The gas-works are now in a forward state, it is expected the town will be lighted up next week. Col. Knox, one of the members, has handsomely given one hundred guineas, which the gas company have laid out in erecting lamp irons and providing lamps for the use of the town. The application of gas is the second move this year in this town. The establishment of a day mail, about six weeks ago, was the first. Marlow may yet rival the great towns in this county.

Newspaper cutting of 1848. Reproduced by courtesy of Marlow Library

ironmonger, tinner and brazier, and registrar of births and deaths. The Company secretary was the ubiquitous William Lakin Ward. In 1848 the vestry decided that the Directors of the Company should sign an undertaking in a letter to Thomas Bowen to restore the 'roadway in several streets' after breaking it up to supply the inhabitants with gas. Six local men were appointed annually as inspectors: in 1850 they were asked to make arrangements with the Gas Company for the better lighting of High Street by increasing the number of lamps from five to seven. They were also to ask about 'the propriety of placing iron posts instead of lamp irons in High Street'. In addition it was proposed that a lamp should be erected to light Potlands and another at the corner 'leading to Thomas Matthews' house'. This was Prospect House in Chapel Street, used in 1851 as a boarding school. The list of men appointed as inspectors in 1851 is in the minutes; they were George Cannon, George Kidd, John Morgan, George Lovegrove, Samuel King and Samuel Harrad, whose name also appears spelt Horrod.

From this short account it is clear that the affairs of the town were being run by a small group of well-to-do traders and craftsmen. Apart from Samuel Horrod, who was retired and who was included in the Directories under

139

West Street c.1896 showing the corner of Quoiting Square; the White Lion sign can be seen on the right and the lamp bearing the Red Lion sign on the left. The gas lamp 'to light Potlands' is on the left at the entrance to the alley, now Portlands Alley by the car-park. Photograph by H.W. Taunt, reproduced by courtesy of Buckinghamshire County Museum

gentry, all the men listed as inspectors had their own businesses. Cannon had a finger in most happenings in the town as well as being churchwarden for the parish, John Morgan was a respected draper, Kidd and Lovegrove were both grocers and Samuel King was another draper. Robert Maddocks, the other churchwarden, was builder and joiner. Normally the men listed as gentry in the Directories do not seem to play any part in the affairs of the vestry.

Sources

Churchwardens' Account Book, 1831-1917, Buckinghamshire County Record Office PR 140/5/4.
Colvin, H.M., 'The Architectural History of Marlow and its Neighbourhood' in *Records of Bucks.* 15, 1947, 5-19.
Minute Book of Great Marlow Vestry, 1846-1896, Wycombe District Council.
Surveyors of the Highways' accounts, 1852-53, Buckinghamshire County Record Office PR 140/21/5.

Charities, the Poor Law, the Union and the workhouse

Before the Poor Law Amendment Act of 1834 the relief of the poor was governed by Elizabethan legislation. Under this parishes were responsible for their poor people; they were required to register them and to nominate overseers, who were appointed annually by the justices of the peace. The overseers saw that the poor law was administered and were also responsible for levying the poor rate.

In addition, many people endowed charities to alleviate the suffering of poor people; more often than not this was done by leaving a property, a house or piece of land, which could be let to produce an annual income to pay for whatever form the charity took.

Great Marlow was blessed with several charities and these are listed in the churchwardens' accounts for 1851. Thomas Drew, who died in 1651, had left land in Islington which produced an annual income of £10 – £11. He had decreed that this sum should be spent on apprenticeships and in 1851 it is recorded:

> *Richard Walker apprenticed to Stephen Harris,*
>   *carpenter in High Wycombe*   *£1.0s.0d.*
> *John Clarke Truss*
>   *to Mr John Middlemost,*
>   *shoemaker, Reading*   *£5.0s.0d.*
> *George Smith*
>   *to Mr Thomas J Langley,*   *£5.0s.0d.*
>   *to the ship 'Lancastrian',*
>   *St Catherine's Docks*

In addition, Thomas Drew's Charity, administered by T.P. Williams, provided £2 12s. for bread which was given monthly to poor people.

The Reverend John Cleobury, who had been vicar of Great Marlow, had left the dividend on £100 invested at 3% to be spent on flannel waistcoats and gowns, to include a payment to the parish clerk for his trouble in having the garments made. Payments were made through Thomas Rolls, who seems to have bought in the flannel.

Paid Messrs Rolls for Flannel	*£1.13s.3d.*
Paid For making garments	*7s.0d.*
Paid Parish Clerk	*5s.0d.*
Paid balance as below	*14s.9d.*

3 waistcoats 3 gowns 5 at 2s.6d. + 2s.3d.

Robert Boothby's Charity, administered by T.P.Williams, paid ten distressed tradesmen ten payments of one shilling, a total of ten shillings a year. Those who benefited in 1851 were:

Joseph Bird	not in the census returns
Richard Bye	aged 73, lodging in Spittal Street, retired
Richard East	aged 77, living in Dean Street, pauper
Abraham Gray	aged 85, living in Forty Green, retired farm labourer
Joseph Green	aged 77, living in Dean Street, farm labourer
William Gunnell	aged 70, living in Oxford Lane, retired
John Harbroe	not in the census returns
William James	aged 72, living in West Street, pauper
William Smith	aged 72, living in West Street, brewer's labourer
Joseph Tilby	aged 48, living in West Street, farm labourer

Other charities included Agnes Friar's – or Fryar's – Charity, by which money received from the rent of two cottages near the Free School was used to pay one shilling to each of twenty widows at Easter. Again the Charity was administered by Thomas Rolls.

The Free School, also known as Borlase School and now as Sir William Borlase School, was established by Sir William Borlase about 1624. In 1628, when he signed the codicil to his will, which provided money for the school which he had already set up, he also stipulated:

That the house where now Hugh Tanner dwelleth adjoyning to ye said Schoolhouse with ye Barne.... shall be for ever employed as a workhouse and House of Correction for ye said three parishes (Great Marlow, Little Marlow and Medmenham) and none other than the said Hugh Tanner and his successors shall be chosen into the place accordingly as ye schoolmaster is hereby appointed to be chosen ... He shall teach yearly 24 women children of the Burrough of Great Marlow only to make bone lace to spin or to knitt.... And the said Hugh Tanner or his successors shall whipp or cause to be whipped all such offenders as ye Petty Constables Officers or Tythingmen of any of the said parishes shall bring to him which by the laws of this realm are to be whipped for any offences so punishable.... And shall keep for four days in his House of Correction any Rogue or vagabond taken within the town or parish of Great Marlow Little Marlow or Medmenham....

This, then, was Marlow's first workhouse.

No papers could be found which explain the origins of the 'lands called Berwicks, lying on the east side of Deane Lane' although a study of all the Marlow charities suggests that this land may be part of the Hawes Charity, probably included under the general charities of the parish. Sometime in the seventeenth century 'poor lands' called Barracks or Berwicks were being let by the overseers and it was on part of this land that the new Marlow workhouse was built in the middle of the eighteenth century. Part of the buildings still stand today in Berwick Road.

Part of the old workhouse building, now converted into private cottages. Photograph by Peter Diplock, 1991

By the beginning of the nineteenth century poor women and girls were still being taught the arts of lace making and their work was sold, quite profitably, until either the fashion for wearing lace went into decline and the demand for it therefore dropped or the competition from cheaper, machine-made lace proved too strong. Men and boys were hired out to work for the Surveyors on highway maintenance and in the workhouse garden. The workhouse accounts for 1819 show that women working in the laundry were being paid 2d. and 3d. each, while men were paid amounts varying from 1d. to 1s.5d. or, if working for the Surveyors, between 3d. and 2s. It is not clear how much work these payments represented. Other payments were made to the surgeon who attended the sick and to the midwife who attended women in

143

childbirth. For example, the churching of Ann Perry and the baptising of her child cost 1s.; when Ann Langley was married, the cost of the ring was 3s.6d. and Mr Badger received 9s. matrimonial fees in his capacity as parish clerk.

The accounts do not include any expenditure for the day-to-day running of the workhouse since it seems to have been the practice to contract out for this. In 1799 it was:

> *Resolved that the Churchwardens and the Overseers do Contract with Mr James Jackson for maintenance, cloathing and employment of the poor of this town and parish for the term of three years certain, at the sum of £1200 a year to be paid by twelve equal payments commencing from the 29th day of September next.*

The Overseers were also responsible for the relief of those poor people who were still able to live in the community. This out-relief took the form of allocations of bread, usually in 4lb loaves, and small money payments 'upon sudden and Emergent occasions'. Life was particularly hard for such people in the winter when there was little casual work to be had. In 1801, known to have been a very bad year, records show that over £50 was paid out in relief over the winter, compared with £9.3s.9d. for the months of July, August and September.

The passing of the Poor Law Amendment Act in 1834 changed all this. Parishes were compulsorily amalgamated into Unions for the purpose of granting poor relief. Marlow became part of the Wycombe Union and, along with the other parishes in the Union, elected representatives to the newly-established Board of Guardians. This body made broad decisions about the running of the workhouse and the management of poor relief and also took decisions about individuals, both in and out of the workhouse. The Guardians met more or less fortnightly, in the workhouse, and the Master reported to them and also the Relieving Officers, each of whom covered a group of parishes with the duty of dealing with those receiving help, or relief, outside the workhouse. Before the 1834 Act, when poor relief was very much a concern for each parish acting individually, Overseers were appointed by the vestry each year with approval from the Justices of the Peace to levy a poor rate and to supervise its distribution. With the establishment of Boards of Guardians some of the duties of the Overseers were handed over to them but local men were still appointed as assessors and collectors of the poor rate, as mentioned in the section on the Church and the Vestry, and also as Relieving Officers.

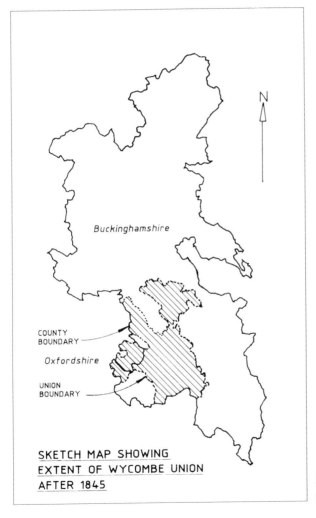

Map showing the extent of Wycombe Union after 1845. Drawn by Joan Rogers

The area covered by the Wycombe Union was very large and Wycombe's own existing workhouse was quite

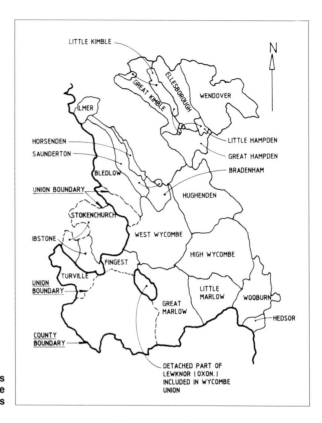

LITTLE KIMBLE

N

GREAT KIMBLE

ELLESBOROUGH

WENDOVER

ILMER

HORSENDEN

SAUNDERTON

LITTLE HAMPDEN

GREAT HAMPDEN

BRADENHAM

BLEDLOW

UNION BOUNDARY

HUGHENDEN

STOKENCHURCH

IBSTONE

WEST WYCOMBE

HIGH WYCOMBE

FINGEST

TURVILLE

UNION
BOUNDARY

LITTLE
MARLOW

WOOBURN

GREAT
MARLOW

HEDSOR

COUNTY
BOUNDARY

DETACHED PART OF
LEWKNOR (OXON.)
INCLUDED IN WYCOMBE
UNION

Map showing the parishes making up the Wycombe Union. Drawn by Joan Rogers

inadequate, so initially the workhouses at Marlow and Bledlow were used. Neither of these was adequate on its own and for some time the Guardians toyed with the idea of extending one of them. Marlow could hold 200 people, according to a report made to the Commissioners in 1842, so it must have been over full when the 1841 census was taken, recording a population of 214. Bledlow, which had been enlarged and repaired, was capable of accommodating 120, so the total number which could be housed in the Wycombe Union at that time was 320. Although, under the 1834 Act, outdoor relief was supposed to cease, the inadequacy of Wycombe's workhouses in 1841 meant that the Clerk to the Wycombe Union, Mr Charles Harman, reported giving outdoor relief to 152 adults and 258 children in the first three weeks of the quarter ending on Lady Day in that year because the workhouse was full. Amongst these were 54 adults and 98 children from Great Marlow. A typical entry reads:

> *Great Marlow   Thomas Frith 46 wife 47 : 5*
> *children*
> *given 4 loaves and 2s.*
>
> *Samuel Terry 40 wife 39 : 6*
> *children*
> *given 8 loaves and 4s.*

But already plans were afoot for a new Union workhouse which was to be built at Saunderton. Ten acres of land had been bought and a contract signed for the erection of a workhouse to house 350 people. Great Marlow wanted to have nothing to do with this new workhouse and suggested that the parish should opt out.

Wycombe Union workhouse at Saunderton, c.1844. Drawn by Margaret Richardson after an artist's impression

It failed to elect members to the Board of Guardians in 1842, which may have been a form of silent protest. Mr Harman wrote to the Commissioners:

> *Great Marlow returns two Members of Parliament and the return at the late election was petitioned against and all the parish officers with their rate books etc. were detained in London for several weeks.*
> *Seven qualified persons having been duly nominated.... I caused the voting papers to be printed but the overseers had not prepared the usual list of persons entitled to vote. Understanding this to be the case and knowing the party feeling in Marlow was being carried on to a very unpleasant extent, I proceeded there on 19th March and went personally to the*

> *residences of the four overseers and the two churchwardens.... all the officers away from home.*

By early in 1843 the new workhouse at Saunderton was finished and in the first week of April in that year relief was being given to 4,055 people – 330 in the workhouse and 3,725 outside. The idea that workhouses were not meant to be attractive places is born out by the details of the diet for the inmates. Quite apart from the boredom it must have represented, it can hardly be described as balanced. Able-bodied men and women were allowed 6oz. of bread at breakfast and at supper each day together with either 1oz. of cheese or 1.2oz of butter. Dinner also consisted of bread and cheese on four days of the week, with meat pudding and vegetables on Sundays and suet pudding with vegetables on Tuesdays and Fridays. Those described as infirm had gruel for breakfast on three days of the week and soup or broth for dinner on three days, suet dumplings on Mondays and cooked meat with vegetables on Tuesdays, Thursdays and Saturdays.

In July 1844 the Poor Law Commissioners were told:

> *that at Michaelmas last the Guardians ceased to occupy the workhouse at Great Marlow, the parish authorities have put some persons in to take care of it, but at present have taken no steps with a view to sale – I believe there are some hostile claims with respect to it.*

It seems that the parish authorities retained the old workhouse for some years. During the years 1844-53 William Crouch or his executors were paying rent to the churchwardens, initially for the workhouse field and then for both the field and the house. The 1851 census shows that eleven families were living in the 'late workhouse'. There seems to be no evidence that they were paying any rent and since they would not have been liable for rates there is no means of knowing whether or not the Poor Law Commissioners knew of their presence. Perhaps they gave up the struggle or simply overlooked the fact that Great Marlow had not sold its old workhouse and paid over the money so obtained.

During 1851/52 various builders were paid for repair work to the house and in 1853 eight tenants were paying rents varying from 6d. to 1s.4d. per week for accommodation in the workhouse cottages. Eventually the administration of the property was taken over by the Oxford United Charities Trust and the cottages continued to be let until they were sold in 1939. The building at Bledlow remained in use for many years, first for housing destitute children and then, in the 1860s, as the school for the Wycombe Poor Law Union.

Interplay between the Great Marlow vestry and the much bigger Board of Guardians is recorded in the vestry minutes in 1850. The Relieving Officer who was responsible for the poor of Great Marlow actually lived in the town. The Board of Guardians decided that two extra parishes – Bledlow and Chinnor – should be added to his district. The vestry thought that, as Bledlow was fifteen miles away and Chinnor seventeen, George Painter, the officer concerned, would have to move and they did not want this to happen. They knew that another of the Relieving Officers lived at Princes Risborough, which was much nearer to Bledlow and Chinnor. So the meeting 'earnestly requested' the Board of Guardians to reconsider and 'make such alterations as will enable a Relieving Officer at all times to reside in the Town of Great Marlow'. This resolution was forwarded to the Board of Guardians together with a request that the Marlow Guardians should come to a vestry meeting. This did, in fact, happen in that James Franklin, a farmer and Guardian, attended the next vestry meeting and reported that an Assistant Poor Law Commissioner had attended the meeting of the Board of Guardians and had told them that the Poor Law Commissioners had refused to sanction the proposal to add Bledlow and Chinnor to the area of Great Marlow's Relieving Officer. So the vestry won on that occasion and George Painter's name appears in the 1851 Rate Book.

Painter had been appointed in December 1845 at a salary of £100 a year, even though his predecessor, Mr Hill, had printed a notice setting out his complaints about the inadequacy of his pay. He had to pay Land Tax and other taxes out of it, and maintain a horse to enable him to cover the area for which he was responsible, as well as provide for himself and his family. Mr Hill resigned in November 1845 in debt, as was the previous Relieving Officer, Joseph Reading, who had resigned in October 1842 owing £112 18s.6d. At the time of his resignation the Board of Guardians said that his default was because the job was beyond his capabilities. There is no evidence as to how George Painter managed, but he was appointed on the same salary as Mr Hill so the latter's complaint had had no effect.

On another occasion a meeting was called by the churchwardens, Robert Maddocks and Thomas Rolls, and the overseers, John Williams and Henry Corby, to discuss the idea of asking the Board of Guardians for 'the appointment of a fit and proper person to be Collector of the Poor Rates for this Parish'. An amendment opposed the idea, stating that the time was not right for such an appointment and although six people supported the amendment Ralph Spicer, solicitor and a member of the Board of Guardians, demanded a poll. Rather like the one called over the rate, this poll began on the same day and ran on the following day until four o'clock. The result was that 113 people were in favour of the idea and 46 were against. So the vestry decided to make the application, suggesting at the same time that the Collector should be paid £30 a year and that Henry Stallwood, an active member of the vestry, would be a 'fit and proper person' for the appointment. The duties of the Collector were listed as:

> to make out all the Poor Rates, lists of voters and the jury list
> to attend all vestries in connection with the Poor Laws
> to keep the accounts
> to collect the Poor Rates and Loans and pay the same when collected at Messrs Wheelers' Bank at High Wycombe to the credit of the churchwardens and overseers of this Parish weekly.

Although there is no direct evidence of the result of this request in that nothing is said in the vestry minutes while the minutes of the Board of Guardians for that year have not been traced, nevertheless the census return does list 'collector of the poor rate' against Henry Stallwood's name.

Two years earlier, in 1848, the vestry decreed that the churchwardens and overseers should raise £96.10s. as a fund to pay the expenses of those 'who have settlement here' to emigrate if they were willing to do so. The question of settlement was an important one. A stranger

Extract from the Minutes of a Meeting of the Board of Guardians of the Wycombe Union held in the Board Room of the Union Workhouse in the Parish of Saunderton on Monday July 30th 1849.

The Clerk reported that Mr Colbourne had made the following note in his Medical Return "Asiatic Cholera has made its appearance here I have seen two decided cases which have terminated fatally in a few hours. We have many Nusiances existing in this Town of a dangerous character which must be immediately removed."

Resolved that the following Guardians be appointed a Committee to inspect the various Nusiances in Great Marlow, namely Mess.rs Franklin Capper, Gaskell, Gibbons, (of Marlow) Musgrave and Harman; and that such Committee be authorized to take such measures as they may deem expedient, for the abatement and removal of such nuisances,

Resolved that Mr Henry Stallwood be appointed an Officer of this Board, to act under the instructions of such Committee.

By the Board

J. Harman,

Clerk of the Union,

Extract from the minutes of the Board of Guardians. Public Record Office staying in a parish could be removed by the overseer if he had no prospect of work within forty days, or if he did not rent property worth £10 a year. So an agricultural labourer, coming to a parish temporarily during harvest, had to bring a certificate with him guaranteeing that his home parish would take him back again. If he could find work for forty days then he could claim that he was settled and could then become a charge on the poor rate if need arose. The following year the vestry decided that Hector Oxlade, his wife and three children should be helped to emigrate to Australia and that they should be allowed 'such sum as the Poor Law Commissioners shall order out of the Great Marlow Fund now in the hands of the trustees of the Wycombe Board of Guardians'. The Oxlade family was granted £25 and were due to sail on the Joseph Soames on 15 August 1850 to North Adelaide in Australia. Records show that the number of people who emigrated from Britain in 1850 was 280,849, more than a threefold increase from 1840 when the number was 90,743. The majority of those emigrating went to the United States, but some went to Australia where the Gold Rush was in full swing.

The sad story of one settlement case was recorded in the *Bucks Advertiser and Aylesbury News* for 5 July 1851:

> *John Hewett, one of the churchwardens of Hambleden, was charged with assisting in the removal of a poor person from that parish to the parish of Great Marlow, he not having obtained an order of removal. It appeared that a girl of the name of Fletcher had loved too well, and was likely to be troublesome, and the parties in whose service she then was being desirous to get rid of her, not wishing for an increase in the establishment, Mr Hewett was consulted, and a plan was set on foot to send her to Marlow forthwith, in her mistress' cart; Mr Hewett consented to accompany the party. The poor unfortunate, when at Marlow, had some difficulty in obtaining lodging, but Mr Hewett resolved to leave her with a poor person, directing her to do her best to obtain lodgings, and gave the girl a shilling, by direction of her late mistress, to pay for her bed. The girl shortly after applied to the relieving officer for*

*assistance. The particulars having been made
known to the Wycombe board, they directed
their clerk to proceed against Mr Hewett, and he
was fined 40s. and costs, for assisting in the
removal from his own parish, whereby the party
became chargeable to Marlow.*

The changes in the provision for the poor which
took place during the first half of the nineteenth century
were considerable. The responsibility was removed from
the individual parish and the new system, more
bureaucratic in nature, was intended to be both more
efficient and also less costly. Workhouses were designed
to be unattractive places so that people would do their
level best not to become inmates. Not everyone approved
of the new arrangements, however, and the following
letter, taken from the *Bucks Advertiser and Aylesbury
News* for 19 April 1851, is worth quoting in full:

Mr Editor

*Permit me, through the instrumentality of your
philanthropic and independent paper, to ask the
professed Christian public what they are
thinking about, in permitting such a monster of
oppression as the New Poor-Law, without lifting
up their voice against it? I think it is high time
that we began to think a little about this monster
of iniquity, and not only to think but to protest
against it. This I believe is the duty of every man
professing Christianity, for the New Poor-Law is
a disgrace to the land we live in, it makes one
ashamed to own he is an Englishman. Its a
downright outrage on humanity. It is a disgrace
to every human feeling. This God dishonouring
and most accursed law was horrible enough at
first, but the longer it is suffered without
interruption the worse it gets. Only think, Sir, for
a moment of what a poor fellow-creature's
feelings must be who has had a good character
all his days, a good straight- forward honest
man; but it is so ordered that he gets out of work,
which is very often the case with farmers
labourers, for I think sometimes there are as
many out of work as there are in work, about
this part of the country; I say only think, for a
moment, what his feelings must be. He goes to
all the farmers and asks for a job. He can't get
one. He is destitute, not a farthing in the world.
He goes to the relieving-officer and the only way*

whereby a mite of relief is to be obtained is to have the degrading answer of a 'Ticket for the Union', where he must be severed from his wife and family, who are as dear to him as his own heart's blood. Here he is shut up in the hands of those who, generally speaking, are destitute of all human feeling. He is driven away from his own happy home into a place of complete misery. Why not give the poor man an allowance out of the workhouse and let him eat his morsel at home, in quietness, with his beloved wife and tender babes? 'Spoil not his resting-place, O wicked man'.

So much for the New Poor-Law, as touching the honest, but unfortunate, labouring man. Now, Sir, a word or two on the system as regards the old and infirm. A little time back the old people who were past labour, in this locality, used to have 3s. and three loaves of bread per week. This was the allowance for a man and his wife, for old disabled people, and those that are past 60 years of age. I know that there were some who had 6d. more than this, here and there one, but 3s. and three loaves of bread were the general allowance. Now, I would like to ask our kind-hearted guardians!! (falsely so called) how these old men and women are to lay this money out so as to keep their poor bodys and souls together. Three shillings, Sir! Well, out of this there is 1s. to pay for rent, and, in many instances, 1s.2d. Then there are 2s., and in some cases only 1s. 10d., to buy coals, wood, candles, soap, tea, sugar, meat, and all the other necessaries of life. I hesitate not in saying this is not sufficient; but I should not have troubled you with my scribble, Sir, but for a more demon-like piece of oppression that came out of our tender-hearted guardians last week! They have taken off, from what I have mentioned above, the sum of 3d., 6d., and, in some cases,, 9d per head. Now, Sir, there are men to advocate all sorts of subjects, and shall it be said that Old England has not a party to advocate the cause of the poor and needy. O Englishmen! let it not be said by one solitary individual, as in the days of old, 'I beheld the tears of such as were opressed, and they had no comforter, and on the side of their opressors there was power, but they

154

had no comforter'. Sir, I think this is a subject that demands the serious consideration of all benevolent people, especially Christians and ministers. This, Sir, would become them far more than the aggression of the Pope, or, I would say, the Popish aggression meetings. If we were to have a few meetings and draw up a few petitions to Parliament, for the abolition of this God-dishonouring and most accursed new Poor-Law, I think we should be acting more philanthropic than taking part with one persecuting man-made church against another. Let the clergy, and the Pope, and his priests, fight that out; that is all only a question of loaves and fishes, but the other is a subject fit for an Englishman. But, for the present, I will conclude, hoping some more able Christian brother than I am will take the matter up, and may it please God to make it a matter of interest to all benevolent and Christian people.

Yours etc.

A Lover of Humanity
Haddenham, April 8, 1851.

Some seventeen years after the 1834 legislation this letter shows that the issue of the care of the poor was still very much alive.

Sources

Lease of Barwicks Poor Lands 1677 and 1688, Buckinghamshire County Record Office PR 140/25/2 and 140/25/3.
Churchwardens' Account Book 1831-1917, Buckinghamshire County Record Office PR 140/5/4.
Minute Book of the Board of Guardians of Wycombe Union, Buckinghamshire County Record Office G/7/1-3.
Minute Book of Great Marlow Vestry, 1848-1856, Wycombe District Council.
Sir William Borlase School papers.
Sparkes, I., *The Book of High Wycombe*, 1979.
Musson and Craven *Directory for Buckinghamshire* 1853.
Pigot and Co., *Directory of Great Marlow* for 1842.
Poor Law Board Correspondence 1847-1849, Public Record Office MH 12/531.
Post Office *Directory for Great Marlow*, Bucks 1864.
Slater's (late Pigot) *Royal National Commercial Directory and Topography* 1851.

Education

Sir William Borlase, of Westhorpe, Little Marlow, founded his Free School in 1624 in memory of his son Henry – who had been an MP for Marlow. The original building still stands in West Street among the many later additions. The codicil to Sir William's will of 1628 refers to this house which he had built and to houses and land

General view of West Street c.1896, showing Sir William Borlase School on the right beyond the house where Shelley once lived. Photograph by W.H. Taunt; reproduced by courtesy of Buckinghamshire County Museum

which he had bought in Great Marlow to be employed for charitable uses for the benefit of the poor of Great Marlow, Little Marlow and Medmenham. The income from these houses and lands amounted at the time to £14 a year and Sir William gave instructions that four hundred pounds should be used by his executors for purchases to produce a further income of £20 a year. The school was to be managed by twelve feoffees or governors, eight from Great Marlow, three from Little Marlow and one from Medmenham and the Lord of the Manor of Danvers in Little Marlow was to be the overall governor. Twenty-four poor boys between the ages of ten and fourteen years, whose parents or friends were not able to pay their school expenses, were to be taught 'to read and write and cast accounts'. From amongst these the six ablest were to be selected, once they were competent in the subjects to be taught, to be given forty shillings apiece towards binding them as apprentices to some trade. The vacancies caused were to be filled by the feoffees so that the school should always, as far as possible, have the statutory twenty-four pupils. The feoffees were also to provide a free house for the schoolmaster, who was to be paid £12 a year, and two reams of paper a year for each of the pupils in addition to their books and whatever other materials were required.

As we have seen, an adjoining cottage on the west side of the house was to be used as a workhouse and 'House of Correction' and the will provided for its

An earlier view of the school showing the workhouse and 'House of Correction'. Reproduced by Alan Holmes from an earlier photograph

occupant to receive £6 to £8 a year in salary, at the discretion of the feoffees. There is some doubt as to when the school for girls, also included in the codicil to Sir William's will, was actually started.

Some of the early records of the school have been lost, perhaps during troubles over the administration in the early eighteenth century, but fortunately many of the later accounts and papers have been preserved. In April 1868 Henry Badger, parish clerk in 1851, is recorded as taking out and re-assembling 'the whole of the papers in the Free School Chest from 1815 to the present time'. The papers have recently been arranged and listed and are now in the County Record Office. Study of them provides an illuminating picture of the school from 1750 onwards.

In 1851 Borlase was still known as the Free School as it always had been and the children still wore the traditional blue cloaks for church parade on Sundays. These cloaks were always made in the town from materials supplied by various outfitters. The bill shows that John Morgan sent in his account on 29 August 1851 for 22 yards of cloaking at 2/3 a yard, binding and cotton and eyes. The bill is receipted as having been paid on 14 April 1852 by Thomas Rolls, one of the feoffees of the school.

Copy of John Morgan's account. Reproduced from the Borlase papers

Sir William Borlase School in 1991. Drawn by Margaret Richardson

Mr Charles Wethered, cousin to the brewers Owen and Lawrence William, had been appointed as headmaster in 1844. In 1849 it is recorded that he advised the feoffees to delay the assembling of the school because of the prevalence of fever in the town, presumably cholera, an interesting sidelight on local conditions. He died in November 1850 and a lawyer's clerk, Mr Edwin Segrave, was appointed to succeed him. According to the

Copy of another account, again showing a considerable delay in payment. Reproduced from the Borlase papers

census returns Mr Segrave was thirty-three; he and his wife, who was a year younger than her husband, had four young children. He held the post of headmaster for thirty years and drew a pension for many years after retirement.

Catherine Camden, wife of Steadman Camden who was a shoemaker, was mistress of the 'blue school girls' at the time and was responsible for making their blue cloaks and also their straw hats. Plans were being made for the closure of the girls' school because of the decline in the bone-lace trade and in 1853 payments were made for girls and infants attending the National Schools in Quoiting Place and Church Passage. Although the possibility of establishing an infants school at Borlase had been considered this had never actually happened.

In the nineteenth century the Trustees were always short of money. There had been a costly law case in the eighteen thirties over a libellous headmaster which nearly ruined the charity. The headmaster's salary and, later, poor Mr Segrave's pension, were under constant review but nevertheless a considerable loan from the Wethered family was repaid over 1851/2 with interest. By 1854 the accounts became more businesslike with regular submissions to the newly-formed Charity Commissioners. Many of the school buildings needed constant repair and the school accounts of the period show many payments to local tradespeople and builders, including both Corby and Bond.

The school still owned property as set out in the will, including a farm at Bix, and derived its income from the rents but again there was constant worry over repairs. At one time the cesspool at the back of the houses in Chapel Street owned by the school became so full, foul and offensive that Wycombe Union served notice that 'immediate measures be taken for abatement' under the Nuisances Removal and Disease Prevention Act 1848.

In 1849 William Walker became a pupil and he provided a graphic description of life at the school. The following extract is taken from J.C.Davies' book on the history of Borlase.

Cottages in Chapel Street built by the feoffees to produce income for the running of the school. The inscription reads:

These Tenements belong To the Free School founded by Sr WILLIAM BORLASE And were built in the year 1755.
Photograph by Peter Diplock, 1991

> *Mr Charles Wethered was Master when my Father took me to him at Easter 1849 when I was nearly nine years old. There were 24 Borlasian or Blue Boys, and he was allowed to have 24 boys who paid a shilling a week and had to find all books, etc. The Blue Boys did not find anything except slate pencils. We wrote with a quill pen, which he showed us how to make.*

WYCOMBE UNION,
IN THE COUNTIES OF
Buckingham and Oxford.

To *The Trustees* _____ of *The Free School* _____

In the Parish of *Great Marlow* in the County of Bucks.

Nuisances Removal and Diseases Prevention Act, 1848.

a Cesspool at the back of Houses in Chapel Street. full foul and offensive

Whereas on the Premises *of which you are owners* situate in the said Parish of *Great Marlow* there exists certain Nuisances stated in the margin hereof, contrary to the Provisions of the above Statute, and to the directions and regulations of the General Board of Health of and prejudicial to the health of parties living in the neighbourhood, and the same having been this day inspected by a Committee of the Guardians of the said Union, duly appointed for such purpose; **I hereby Give you Notice**, that unless the said Nuisances be forthwith abated, and all cause of complaint in respect thereof forthwith removed, immediate measures will be adopted by the said Committee for the abatement and removal thereof, and proceedings taken against you for the recovery of the costs of such abatement and removal, and of the penalties by you incurred.

Dated this *Eleventh* — day of *February* — 1849*57*

Henry Hallwood

OFFICER APPOINTED BY THE SAID GUARDIANS IN THIS BEHALF.

Copy of the notice served by the Board of Guardians, who were responsible for community health. Reproduced from the Borlase papers

When we first went to school we made our own writing books. The big boys would go into the Master's kitchen, and, with his housekeeper, make the books from great sheets of paper. There were four large desks in the Schoolroom, two for Blue Boys and two for Day Boys. The Head Boy (monitor) sat at the end of the desk and each class had to learn the same lesson, for which the monitors were responsible, and if we did not do our work we were 'bumped' by the other boys. We used to line up every morning for Scripture. On Fridays we had collects, gospels and catechism, and the same on Sundays. On Mid Lent Sunday afternoon we had to go to Church to be examined by the Vicar and the Trustees.

William Walker was one of the boys selected for apprenticeship. He was apprenticed to Joseph Green, wheelwright, who was living in Chapel Street. Joseph was sixty-three at the time of the census and had probably been married twice; he had a daughter of thirty-three and then three young children under five. His wife was over twenty years younger than he was. The £2 from the Free School formed only part of the apprenticeship costs: Joseph Green also received £6 from Loftin's Charity and £4 from Thomas Walker, William's father, who was a furniture-broker. The Walker family lived in Market Square, next to the Crown Hotel, and William, who was ten at the time of the census and was described as a scholar, had two brothers and four sisters. His eldest brother was an apprentice cabinet-maker and his younger brother was only four. Of the girls, one was a dressmaker, one a house servant and two were at school.

To return to the apprenticeship, William had to promise to serve from the day on which it started until he was twenty-one. That meant at least seven years in his case. He was not allowed to marry during this period, nor play cards or gamble. Taverns and playhouses were barred and he was not allowed to absent himself from his master's service by day or by night without lawful cause. An apprenticeship was a hard period for a craftsman wishing to qualify in his trade, and William probably earned about two shillings and sixpence a week during the first year and then an increment of sixpence a week, reaching the princely sum of four shillings and sixpence a week at the age of twenty.

In addition to the Free School there were in Marlow in 1851 two minor boarding schools. One was for boys and was housed in Prospect House in Chapel Street. The Preceptor was Thomas Mathews and the eleven boy boarders, ranging in age from seven to fourteen, came from places like High Wycombe, Saunderton, Turville and Watlington. In addition there were day pupils but there is no record of how many. A school for girls was in West Street and was apparently run by Ann Heath according to the Directories. She does not appear in the census returns, which show that Maria Dench was in charge. Miss Dench, who was twenty-one at the time, was probably a relation of Miss Heath. There were two living-in servants and thirteen scholars aged from eleven to seventeen years. The provenance of these girls was much more exotic than that of the boys at Prospect House, ranging from The Cape of Good Hope to Marylebone, Middlesex, and from

Market Harborough to Rotherhithe. Once again there were day pupils.

Apart from these rather middle-class schools there were the schools established under the auspices of the National Society for the Education of the Poor in the Principles of the Established Church. The Society was founded in 1811 and by 1851 it controlled over 17,000 schools. In Marlow the first National School was established, for boys, in 1813 in Church Passage, a similar establishment being set up for girls in the following year. Appeals for funds were occasionally made at the parish church, notable collections being made in 1823 and 1828. The minutes of the boys' school exist for several years and show how the school was set up. After various of the townspeople had subscribed funds for its establishment a master, John Betsworth, was appointed and sent to the Central School in London to be 'trained' in the 'Madras System of Education'. This system was developed by Andrew Bell, amongst others. In 1789 he was appointed chaplain of Fort St George in Madras and also the superintendent of the institution which had been established to provide education for the orphan children of the military personnel. Mr Bell was not able to obtain qualified staff for his school, and probably could not have afforded to pay them anyway, so he introduced the system of older pupils teaching other pupils. This system proved to be successful and Bell wrote a pamphlet about it when he returned to England in 1797 entitled *An Experiment in Education made at the Male Asylum of Madras.*

When Mr Betsworth returned with his certificate a school was immediately set up in his house, rented from T.P.Williams. The first boys were admitted on 27 April 1813, each subscriber who had given half a guinea or more being allowed to propose one boy. Forty-two boys attended on the first day, their ages ranging from five to eleven. As well as going to school on weekdays the boys had to attend church on Sundays and members of the committee of management were appointed as visitors to the school. They also received the report of the headmaster at the church on Sundays. Within a year the number of boys at the school had risen to 129 and the house had to be enlarged. At this time the feoffees of the

Free School approached the committee of the National School with an offer to pay over £4 18s. a year if a school for girls could be established on the Madras System. The ladies of Marlow set about raising funds and the girls' school opened in October 1814. In the December of that year the committee ordered 95lbs. of beef 'and sufficient quantity of Plumbs and currants for puddings, about 13½ gallons of Table Beer and about 200 of 1d. loaves and a sufficient quantity of turnips and carrotts, for the purpose of providing the Boys and Girls with a Dinner on the 26 inst.. And that each Boy and Girl do provide themselves with a plate, knife and fork and a ½ pint jug'.

The minute books of the boys' school exist until 1843 and tell us that Henry Badger, the Parish Clerk in 1851, took over the running of the school in 1838, originally as a temporary measure. He was still there in 1843, though by then the school seems to have been in Quoiting Place. His wife Jane was mistress of the girls' school in 1842 and the census returns show that she still held this post in 1851. The boys were taught reading, based mainly on the Bible and the catechism, and ciphering or elementary arithmetic. Discipline must always have been a problem and Mr Betsworth was told not to use corporal punishment. Persistent truancy or non-attendance was punished by a reprimand after being reported to the committee and this sometimes resulted in 'confinement in the Black Hole for an hour' or even expulsion. From time to time it is reported that boys asked permission to leave to go to work or sometimes to go to the Free School. When this was granted parents were expected to attend the school to thank the committee for their child's schooling. Not surprisingly it was usually the mother who did this. One of Henry Badger's reports records the poor state of the school and at the time of the census a new school was being built on the Causeway. The brass plate recording this can still be seen in the main hall of what is now the Church Hall. This school was still the boys' school in the 1880s and continued to be used as a class room for the girls' school – which was opened, together with the Infants School, in 1869 – until the 1960s. There was also a Catholic School, started as a mixed school in 1845 in St Peter's Street. Two ladies from West

Street, Ellen Williams and her sister, were the teachers in 1851.

It is difficult to establish a more accurate picture of education in Marlow in 1851 and it is important to remember that, at that time, it was not compulsory. The statistics show that there were 547 boys and 472 girls between the ages of five and fourteen in the parish. This is about a quarter of the entire population of 4,423. The census returns vary in the information provided about the children, under the heading 'occupation'; some are listed as 'scholar', a very small number (15) are listed as 'scholar at home', some are given an occupation and for the rest the entry is left blank.

	Boys	Girls
Scholars	307	260
With occupation	93	66
No entry	147	146
total numbers	547	472

Some variations can be seen across the parish.

	Town		Rest of Parish	
	Boys	Girls	Boys	Girls
Scholars	65%	61%	32%	36%
With occupation	10%	9%	25%	19%
No entry	25%	30%	43%	45%

Many of the boys who were said to be working had occupations connected with agriculture. The youngest seems to have been George Blackwell, an eight-year-old, who lived with his family in Lane End. He was entered as an agricultural labourer, as was his father. His brother, a year younger, was entered as scholar. Another common job was that of errand boy.

Amongst the girls, occupations were associated with satin-stitch work, lace making or as seamstresses. The youngest girl who was working seems to have been Sarah Wardle, an eight-year-old lace maker, also living in Lane End with her family. Her father was a chair maker, as was her older brother, and her mother and an older sister were both lace makers.

Of the fifteen children who were listed as 'scholars at home' one lived at Bovingdon Green, five in one household in Oxford Lane and nine in High Street. One of the High Street families was that of Charles Bloxham, living at Cromwell House; the children were Anna aged thirteen, John aged seven and Ann aged six. All three children and their two older sisters had been born in Middlesex and their governess Miss Elizabeth Vaughan was also a Londoner. The other High Street family was that of John Aldridge, a barrister. He and his wife, who was a Marlow girl, had five daughters, ranging in age from five to twelve, only one of whom had been born in the town. There were two governesses, Miss Harriet Brown from Hampshire and Mlle. Angele Alland from France. The Oxford Lane family was that of the Reverend G.H.Peel, an elderly clergyman of the Church of England, who was the father-in-law of both Owen and Florence James Wethered and came from Lancashire. In 1851, aged seventy-two, he lived with another married daughter, Mrs Cox, and his unmarried son. Mrs Cox's family of six also lived with their grandfather, and five of them, aged from five to eleven, were being educated at home by their governess Miss Bradley. Again none of the children had been born in the town. The household was a large one since there were also a cook, two nurses, a butler, a coachman, two housemaids and a kitchen maid. Unfortunately it is not possible to say where in Oxford Lane this family lived; although the census returns give the details already mentioned there is no record of the Peel family or the Cox family in the Rate Book.

Sources

Sir William Borlase School papers.
Davies, J.C., *Borlase 1624-1932*, 1932.
Minute books of the boys' schools established under the auspices of the National Society 1813-1843 (in the care of the Wethered family).

Postscript

This, then, is how we have come to see the town of Great Marlow in the mid-nineteenth century, sometimes clearly, sometimes with uncertainty but always with affection.

We who have worked on this study find that we look at present-day Marlow through new eyes. We hope that you who have read this may also discover an added dimension.

West Street. Drawn by
Margaret Richardson